TEACHER EDUCATION FOR SPECIAL NEEDS IN EUROPE

Marianna Sturridge
Goschen Centre
X5292

Also available from Cassell:

H. Daniels and J. Anghileri: *Secondary Mathematics and Special Educational Needs*
S. Hegarty: *Meeting Special Needs in Ordinary Schools (2nd edition)*
D. Hornby: *Working with Parents of Children with Special Needs*
D. Johnstone: *Further Opportunities*
D. Montgomery: *Children with Learning Difficulties*
B. Norwich: *Reappraising Special Needs Education*
J. Sayer: *Secondary Schools for All (2nd edition)*
J. Stone: *Mobility for Special Needs*
B. Walters: *Management for Special Needs*
S. Wolfendale: *Primary Schools and Special Needs (2nd edition)*
S. Wolfendale (ed.): *Assessing Special Educational Needs*

Teacher Education for Special Needs in Europe

Edited by

Peter Mittler and Patrick Daunt

CASSELL

Cassell
Wellington House   215 Park Avenue South
125 Strand   New York
London WC2R OBB   NY 10003

First published 1995

British Library Cataloguing-in-Publication Data
A catalogue record for this book is available from the British Library.

ISBN 0-304-33405-7 (hardback) 0-0304-33406-5 (paperback)

Acknowledgment

Chapter 1, 'A Comparison of Educational Provision for Pupils with Special Educational Needs in Europe' is adapted from Christine O'Hanlon, 'The European dimension in integration and special needs education', *Research Papers in Education*, **8** (1), published in 1993 by Routledge and reproduced here with their permission.

Typeset by York House Typographic Ltd, London
Printed and bound in Great Britain by Redwood Books Limited, Trowbridge, Wiltshire

Contents

Notes on Contributors

Maria Jesus Balbás is Assistant Lecturer in the Department of Didactics and School Organization, Faculty of Educational Sciences, University of Seville.

Marie Černá is Professor and Head of the Department of Special Education, Faculty of Education, Charles University, Prague.

Gina Conti-Ramsden is Director of the Centre for Educational Needs, School of Education, University of Manchester.

Yvonne Csányi is Professor and Head of the Department for the Education of the Hearing Impaired, Barczi Gusztav College of Special Education, Budapest.

Vasile Chiş is Senior Lecturer in the Department of Educational Sciences, Babes-Bolyai University, Cluj-Napoca.

Patrick Daunt is former Head of the Bureau for Action in Favour of Disabled People of the European Commission, Brussels, and now UNESCO consultant on Special Needs Education to the Romanian Government.

Radu Diaconescu is Director of the Centre for the Development of the Personality of the Child, Craiova.

Garry Hornby is Lecturer in Special Education, School of Education, University of Hull.

Miron Ionescu is Professor and Head of the Department of Educational Sciences, Babes-Bolyai University, Cluj-Napoca.

Mel Johnson is Headteacher of Northcott Special School.

Mike Johnson is Senior Lecturer in Special Education at the Special Educational Needs Centre, Didsbury School of Education, Manchester Metropolitan University.

Angeles Parrilla Latas is Lecturer in the Department of Didactics and School Organization, Faculty of Educational Sciences, University of Seville.

Olof Magne is a Researcher and former Professor in the Department of Educational and Psychological Research, Malmö School of Education, University of Lund.

David Mitchell is Professor of Education and Director of International Programmes at the School of Education, University of Waikato, Hamilton, New Zealand.

Peter Mittler is Professor of Special Education and former Dean and Director of the Faculty of Education, University of Manchester.

Silvia Moniga is a psychologist and PhD researcher in Developmental Psychology at the University of Padua.

Christine O'Hanlon is Senior Lecturer in Special Education and Educational Psychology, School of Education, University of Birmingham.

Patricia Potts is a Lecturer at the Centre for Curriculum and Teaching Studies, School of Education, The Open University.

Stefan Przybylski is Assistant Professor of Education, Maria Grzegorzewska College of Special Education, Warsaw.

Peter D. Pumfrey is Professor of Education at the School of Education, University of Manchester.

Jerry Rosenqvist is Acting Professor of Special Education, Unit of Special Education, Malmö School of Education, University of Lund.

Ingvar Sandling is Senior Lecturer in Special Education, Unit of Special Education, Malmö School of Education, University of Lund.

Monika A. Vernooij is Director of the Institute of Special Education and Dean of the Faculty of Educational Science, Justus-Liebig University, Giessen.

Renzo Vianello is Professor of Developmental Psychology, Department of the Psychology of Development and Socialization, University of Padua.

Mike Wright is Principal Adviser to the Humberside Education Authority.

Foreword

Although a little more information is now available about educational opportunities for children and young people with special educational needs in Europe (Daunt, 1991; Mittler *et al.*, 1993; O'Hanlon, 1993), very little is known about opportunities for training and professional development for their teachers or for other staff with responsibilities for their learning and development.

It was against this background that, with the aid of a grant from the Helios programme of the European Union, the European Association for Special Education (EASE) sponsored an international symposium at the University of Manchester from 6 to 9 July 1993. Approximately 35 participants from over ten European countries met to discuss current trends on teacher education for special educational needs; the organizers were particularly glad to welcome colleagues from Central and Eastern Europe. The experience was felt to be highly informative as well as thought-provoking; many useful contacts were made and a number of ideas for new partnerships were developed during and after the symposium.

Another outcome of the symposium is this book, which is largely derived from the papers presented there, some of them updated or expanded.

It will be clear to any reader of this book, as it was to us who took part in the symposium, that in Europe, while at the level of principles and philosophy there are signs of a trend towards convergence, we are still faced with an enormous diversity in policies, practice and provision.

At one end of the continuum there is Italy, a country with over a decade's experience of full integration, where plans are currently being drawn up to make all teaching a graduate profession. It is planned that special education will be an integral part of the new initial teacher training system. At the other end we have countries such as the Czech Republic, where the Ministry of Education is proposing that 'public schools will be open to everybody, but not for those who require extra special care', and where all teacher education is in need of reform and update, let alone teacher training for special educational needs. As our Czech colleagues said: 'It is not just teachers that need to change but society has to as well, in order that children with special educational needs can be accepted and valued.' At the same time, a country such as the Czech Republic has a rich tradition of humanist ideas which provide a strong philosophical basis for inclusive education and the integration of training for all teachers.

The picture that emerges is not a simple one. It is not the case that Eastern Europe is 'less advanced' and Western Europe 'more advanced'. It appears that we have different strengths in different countries, deeply rooted in history and culture. It is this richness of information to communicate and variety of experience to share that led the participants in the symposium to emphasize how much we can learn from one another.

So is a European view of special educational needs possible? Although diversity may present itself as the first hurdle, it is certainly not an insurmountable one and may turn out not to be a hurdle at all.

Links between different European countries through the ERASMUS and TEMPUS programmes of the European Union, the European Association for Special Education, the Association for Teacher Education in Europe (ATEE) and other organizations, can facilitate understanding and discussion and lead to the transfer of good practice; the results of research and the experience of innovation can be shared. Agreement on principles is both desirable and possible in a more united and equitable Europe – and that means the whole of historical Europe. Wherever common principles are recognized, differences in specific policies, practices and provision, far from being a barrier to fruitful exchange, can become a source of heightened awareness and a challenge to complacency.

Two of the most important of such agreed principles which emerged in the Manchester symposium and which can be clearly perceived in this book are the determination to strive towards the goal of a truly inclusive school and the recognition that special educational needs should be included in the initial and continuing training of all teachers.

The editors would like to thank the authors for their cooperation in the revision of their symposium contributions in order to achieve a book which we hope is reasonably well balanced. We should also like to express our appreciation to our colleagues in the organization of the symposium, in particular to the President and Treasurer of EASE, Klaus Wenz and Bo Rodvig. Of the many people in Manchester who worked to ensure the success of the symposium, and therefore made it possible for this book to be conceived, we should like to single out Averil Gould for all her work to prepare the symposium and the staff at Hulme Hall who provided excellent hospitality and a pleasant and comfortable meeting room. Following the meeting, Jane Reeves worked for many hours to retype the papers and Jean-Ann Naylor helped with translations.

Peter Mittler, Gina Conti-Ramsden and *Patrick Daunt*

REFERENCES

Daunt, P.E. (1991) *Meeting Disability: A European Response*. London: Cassell.
Mittler, P., Brouillette, R. and Harris, D. (eds) (1993) *World Yearbook of Education: Special Needs Education*. London: Kogan Page.
O'Hanlon, C. (1993) *Special Education: Integration in Europe*. London: Fulton.

List of Abbreviations

ACS	Academic Computing Service (of UKOU)
AII	Aptitude and Instruction Interaction
ASE	Association for Special Education, now NASEN
ATEE	Association for Teacher Education in Europe
CEDCP	Centre for the Education and Development of the Child (Romania)
CERI	Centre for Educational Research and Innovation
CIS	Commonwealth of Independent States
CMUDD	Centre Médico-universitaire Daniel Douaday
CNIS	National Coordination of Specialized Teachers and Research on Handicap (Italy)
DECP	Department for Education Code of Practice
DES	Department of Education and Science, now DfE
DfE	Department for Education
EADTU	European Association of Distance Teaching Universities
EASE	European Association for Special Education
EBD	emotional and behavioural learning difficulties
EC	European Community
ECYEB	European Community Youth Exchange Bureau
ETUCE	European Teacher Trade Union Committee for Education
EU	European Union
GEST	grants for educational support and training
HI	hearing impairment
HMI	Her Majesty's Inspectors/Inspectorate
ICIDH	International Classification of Impairments, Disabilities and Handicaps
IET	Institute of Educational Technology (of UKOU)
INSET	in-service education for teachers
ITE	initial teacher education
ITT	initial teacher training
IUFM	Institut Universitaire de la Formation des Maîtres (Grenoble)
LEA	local education authority

LMS	local management of schools
MLD	moderate learning difficulties
MMU	Manchester Metropolitan University
NARE	National Association of Remedial Education, now NASEN
NASEN	National Association for Special Needs
NGO	non-governmental organization
OECD	Organization for Economic Cooperation and Development
OFSTED	Office for Standards in Education
OJEC	Official Journal of the European Communities
PGCE	Postgraduate Certificate in Education
PHARE	Poland and Hungary Aid to Restore the Economy
PMLD	profound and multiple learning difficulties
SDD	specific developmental dyslexia
SEN	special educational needs
SENCO	special educational needs coordinator
SENIOS	special educational needs in ordinary schools
SLD	severe learning difficulties
SPI	Siauliai Pedagogical Institute (Lithuania)
SpLD	specific learning difficulties
TEMPUS	Trans European Mobility Programme for University Staff
TEWG	teacher education working group
TOS	therapy-oriented special education
TTA	Teacher Training Agency
UKOU	United Kingdom Open University
UNESCO	United Nations Educational, Scientific and Cultural Organization
USL	Unità Sanitaria Locale (Italy)
VI	visual impairment

Part I

Overview

Chapter 1

A Comparison of Educational Provision for Pupils with Special Educational Needs in Europe

Christine O'Hanlon

INTRODUCTION

The education process is at the centre of and permeates all community life at both national and international level. As the new educational attitudes within Europe are being formed, we witness in each country's national educational practice, the creation by the European Union (EU) of political safeguards in the form of protective measures for minorities. Children with disabilities and special educational needs (SEN) in the Union are identified as a minority, so essential legislation has been passed at national and international level to guarantee their education and to ensure quality and choice within the education systems.

The observance of human rights in Europe was originally embedded in the Convention for the Protection of Human Rights and Fundamental Freedoms within the Council of Europe, which was signed by the member states as early as 1950. Since that time the preservation of basic human rights has formed the foundation of all measures adopted by the Council of Europe.

The EU does not have the power to prescribe a unified education policy to member states. The EU has wide powers to formulate and implement policy, but individual countries, for example the UK, can opt out of certain policy instruments such as the Social Charter. This allows the UK freedom from its legislation, whereas countries which accept the Charter must carry out any directives based on it.

Although there is no specific EU legislation for integration or inclusive education, there is evidence of the development of similar themes and focuses within member states in relation to the education of pupils with SEN. At present a joint course on education policy is being studied by the Council of Ministers. The Council is advised by various expert committees on schooling, education, higher education, adult education and culture. When deliberations are completed, the Council of Ministers will pass general guidelines for the inclusion of pupils with SEN in education with the recommendation that member states will bear the EU guidelines in mind when passing their own legislation.

In the broader European context in the last decades, our knowledge about SEN provision and integration has increased enormously due to the research carried out by official international organizations such as the United Nations Educational, Scientific and Cultural Organization (UNESCO), the Organization for Economic Cooperation and Development (OECD), the EU and the Council of Europe. Within member states, too, national organizations have contributed through research projects and the publication of professional journals wholly or partly devoted to special education. However, even with such a plethora of information, it is difficult to make international comparisons based on national outlooks. There are few common or normative references for comparisons within and between national education systems in a micro-focus, yet broad directions of change are discernible in both a unitary and a multidimensional macro-European context.

The Maastricht Treaty (1991) acknowledged the responsibility of member states for the organization of their own education systems by restricting EU action in the development of national education systems. Although this offers member states their own educational autonomy through the 'subsidiarity' principle, it does not help to develop the unity and harmonization of educational systems in Europe. A united Europe will act as a challenge to finding a European dimension in education (Rohrs, 1992; Bruce, 1991). In spite of the fact that the concept of the EU will embrace a wider Europe with the imminent accession of countries including Sweden, Norway, Austria and Finland, it is influenced too by the dramatic developments in Central and Eastern Europe. Mulcahy (1991) is reassured that the Community is clearer now than it was in the past on what it means by the European dimension in education.

However, Drucker (1989) warns us that, in spite of the EU's focus on the extension of knowledge, it is the responsibility of educationalists to use moral safeguards in the European drive for a knowledge-dominated workplace and society. In considering students with SEN in Europe we are addressing the themes of human rights and morality as well as the achievement of equal opportunity and full access to all forms of education. The economic and technological development of Europe demands continually rising levels of quality in skills and professions in the new European workforce. This demand must be recognized in the determination of educational aims and resources in member countries.

SPECIAL EDUCATIONAL NEEDS IN EUROPE

One of the initial problems in the discussion of provision for students with SEN in Europe is the importance of understanding one another's language. Apart from the fact that Europe has many different languages there are a number of terms in use which are not translatable into different registers. One example of this is the term 'special educational needs'. As readers will recognize, in the UK this term refers to children with physical and sensory disabilities, and with learning difficulties along a continuum from mild to severe. But in translation the concept becomes problematic. In European working groups generally, it is normal procedure to clarify terminology by using the International Classification of Impairments, Disabilities and Handicaps (ICIDH). This results in the widespread use of the word 'disability' rather than 'handicap', as 'disability' has a definitive and objective nature whereas 'handicap' is seen as the disadvantage incurred by the person through the interaction of a disability and an unresponsive environment. In order to ensure that meanings of different terms are not misinterpreted in member states, the World Health Organization defined the terms thus (EASE, 1990):

- An *impairment* is any loss or abnormality of psychological, physiological or anatomical structure or function.
- A *disability* is any restriction or lack, resulting from an impairment, of ability to perform an activity in the manner or within the range considered normal for a human being.
- A *handicap* is a disadvantage, for a given individual, resulting from an impairment or a disability, that limits or prevents the fulfilment of a role that is normal (depending on age, sex, and social and cultural factors) for that individual.

Even with this situation, the French cannot find in their language an acceptable equivalent to the word 'disabled'; therefore the word 'handicap' is often translated in English from official European documentation written in the French language, although the meaning differs from disability.

BACKGROUND

In the latter half of the nineteenth and the first half of this century, the main form of response to children with SEN was a medical one, with the establishment all over Europe of educational and residential institutes first for 'the deaf' and 'the blind', then for children with 'mental' and 'physical disabilities'

The first 'special schools' were established in France, Switzerland, Scotland and England between 1760 and 1800 (Potts, 1982), very much in line with the gradually developing network of state education. Mass education was introduced in the Elementary Education Act of 1870, followed by legislation in 1890 in England. By 1918 local education authorities (LEAs) were obliged to provide schools or classes for all children defined as educable. Yet the reason behind the establishment of special schools was often linked to eugenics and the removal of unfit or ineducable children from mainstream provision. It was not until 1970 that further legislation in the UK enabled all children to be considered educable and for their schooling, at least, to be provided by an 'education' rather than a 'health' authority. In Europe generally the 1940s, 1950s and 1960s witnessed a dramatic development of legislation aimed at promoting the training and employment of disabled people: this came from the demand from disabled people for equal opportunity in society, and from the widening labour market (Daunt, 1991).

Since 1970 UK legislation, which emanated from the Warnock Report (DES, 1978, later enshrined in the 1981 Education Act), has forged a line of development in the field of SEN that has kept pace and shown a lead to other European countries in making plans for children with SEN. At about the same time as Britain was establishing the practice of integrating SEN pupils into mainstream schools, Europe was making progress with developing its own policies for 'handicapped' children, as they were then called. In 1980 the Commission's Education Division produced a study on the education of children with disabilities in the then European Community, which brought together basic facts and recent information on the subject for the first time. The report also identified ten convergent policy trends which have been influential in the creation of the Commission's own policy (Jørgensen, 1980).

The United Nations International Year of Disabled People (1981) also formed a basis for progress in the EU's response to the social and economic needs of the disabled, and led directly to the establishment of the first action programme, entitled 'The Social Integration of Disabled People – a Framework for Community Action'. It contained the recommendation that member states should 'promote measures to prepare handicapped people for an active life, in particular by integrating them in normal education and training whenever possible'. This first action programme led directly to the second action programme, HELIOS, established in 1988. At the same time as the first programme was being established, the Working Group on Special Education of the Association for Teacher Education in Europe (ATEE) was set up. The working group's central core of members succeeded in grappling with the problems of different concepts and different languages, and grew, through the organization of a series of international conferences and study visits in Amsterdam, Cologne, Belfast, London, Barcelona, Lisbon and Dublin. The issues covered ranged from teacher training to preparation for adult life and integration into the mainstream in a European context (Diniz and Kropveld, 1982, 1984, 1986, 1987, 1989), and the conferences were predominantly funded by the EU's Bureau for Action in Favour of Disabled People. In recent years a series of education networks has also been established through the HELIOS programme in Brussels, one of which is 'The European Dimension in Education, and the Integration of Handicapped Children in School'. The membership is at present small but work is progressing on pupil case studies in Europe and on teacher training for pupils with SEN in special or mainstream settings. Involvement with both groups has enabled me to develop understandings of the complexity of the education of pupils with SEN in Europe.

THE PRESENT SITUATION

There is little to link the diverse systems of education within Europe, especially those aspects of the systems organized specifically for children with SEN. Education is compulsory in all European countries; the starting school age varies between three and seven years, and the total years of schooling from nine to twelve years. If children with SEN are included in the education system, as opposed to the health or social system, then those children are expected to attend schools under the same conditions as other children. Each country has its own form of administration which defines children within a medical or an educational dimension, usually reflected in a national school system leaning predominantly either towards mainstreaming or towards special schooling.

In Eastern Europe, for example, the Czech Republic provides compulsory education for children from the age of 6 to 15 years, yet excludes children who have severe and profound mental retardation from this provision. Approximately 3 per cent of the school-age population are enrolled in special educational provision in special schools. Although the country has no specific policy for the encouragement of educational integration, social integration is the ultimate aim of special or mainstream schooling. Yet it is claimed that the Czech education policy aims to provide a uniform education system with no discrimination against 'handicapped' pupils, who are encouraged to achieve their highest education potential.

Denmark, on the other hand, provides compulsory education for children from the age of 7 to 15 years, including children who have disabilities. Since 1969, schoolchildren in Denmark have been educated in the *folkeskole* which aims to include all children. The Danish Parliament passed a resolution on the reform of education which included the statement:

> The instruction of 'handicapped' pupils shall be extended in such a way that the children can receive instruction in a normal school environment if the parents so wish and can care for the child at home, and if the commitment to an institution is not a necessary part of the treatment.

The subsequent development of the *folkeskole* reflects a remarkably high degree of inclusion. Approximately 13 per cent of school-age children are enrolled in special educational provision generally. Out of approximately 80,000 pupils referred annually to special instruction, almost 70,000, or 87.5 per cent, receive special support in the ordinary school, while 60 per cent of the remaining 10,000 pupils attend special classes in ordinary schools. The country's special education policy is based on three principles:

1. *Normalization.* Every child, regardless of physical or mental handicap, should have the same access to education and training. This is part of a general effort to remove the legislative and institutional barriers facing disabled people in society.
2. *Decentralization.* As many social tasks as possible should be transferred from the state to the region or local municipality, so that local authorities can solve problems at the point where they arise.
3. *Integration.* Integration has not been directly legislated for, but it is promoted indirectly by legal normalization and administrative decentralization and by the provision of the *folkeskole*, that is, comprehensive basic education for all pupils.

In contrast, legislation in the Czech Republic defines categories and degrees of disability. Nine categories of disability are defined: mental retardation, physical disability, emotional disturbance, visual impairment, hearing impairment, language disorder, learning disability, medical/health impairment, and multiple or combined disabilities. The legislation in Denmark does not define categories of disability, yet Ministry of Education regulations specify seven categories used in informing decisions about the placement of pupils: general learning disabilities, emotional disturbance, physical disability, visual impairment, hearing impairment, learning disorders, and reading/learning disabilities (UNESCO, 1988). In these two countries therefore we find differences in forms of categorization, in policies related to integration and in the percentage of the school-age population considered to have SEN.

Among the Scandinavian countries there are also some important differences in practice. In Norway, all children, without exception, are educated from the ages of 7 to 16. Of school-aged children, 0.7 per cent are enrolled in 'special education provision'. Another 3 per cent are in receipt of special education in mainstream schools on a regular basis. Norway's special education policy is to provide equal opportunities for all children in education. Children and young people with disabilities and handicaps have the right to education equal to their abilities, qualifications and interests. When special education is advocated, it is provided in accordance with the principles of normalization and integration.

In Sweden, education is compulsory for all children without exception from the ages of 7 to 16 years, which is similar to Denmark. There are no exact figures for children in special education provision, as there are no boundaries between mainstream and special education, so we cannot make a comparison of the number or percentage of pupils with SEN. Sweden's special education policy is to provide for all children according to need within the framework of an ordinary school. There is provision of a full range of support services in both mainstream and special schools to meet the special needs of all pupils.

In neighbouring Norway the legislation does not define categories of disability, and children with SEN are included in an integral way in recent education laws. There is a very low number of children in segregated special schooling, but it is not possible to make a comparison with the situation in Sweden or other countries. A similar legislative background to that in Sweden exists for the right to inclusion in mainstream schools, although special regulations are included in the general education law for schools for children who are mentally retarded and profoundly deaf.

Finland, too, a close neighbour of Sweden, provides compulsory education for children aged 6 to 16, with no exceptions. Approximately 2.5 per cent of school-age children are enrolled in special education provision, which is higher than in Norway. The policy is to establish a common framework for all schools, where special services are included as a part of the general provision for all pupils. It appears that all three countries aim to provide a common education for all children with different criteria for their selection and for their support.

The legislation in Finland does not define categories of disability, although for curriculum purposes four groups are identified: mildly mentally retarded, moderately and severely mentally retarded, profoundly mentally retarded, and deaf children. The general educational legislation includes children with disabilities, except for severely disabled children, who are governed by the law for the special care of disabled children. The Ministry of Social Affairs and the National Board for Social Welfare are responsible for the education of mentally retarded children, but advice and supervision of teachers is provided by the Ministry of Education and the National Board of General Education. Finland differs from its neighbours in treating severely and profoundly disabled children separately in legislation and policy administration, as was formerly the case in the UK, the Netherlands and Belgium. Few European countries today provide education for children with special needs under the Department or Ministry of Health or Social Welfare. That the education of children with SEN is normally included under the management of education departments indicates a significant change of attitude, from the emphasis on care to education for all children.

Let us further examine legislative practice and policy in the EU, in particular in the Netherlands and Germany, to illustrate the diversity of systems and policies in a range of European countries.

In the Netherlands, all children must attend school between the ages of 5 and 16 years. Approximately 7 per cent of all pupils were enrolled in special educational provision in the 1980s, an increase from 3 per cent in the 1960s (Heyning and Kropveld, 1989). Special education policy in the Netherlands is ostensibly to educate all children in mainstream schools as far as possible. Children are not encouraged to remain for their school lives in a special school unless it is absolutely necessary and they must be integrated into mainstream provision as soon as possible. In preparation for this, mainstream schools are provided with the resources and expertise necessary to teach all children with special needs. The legislation defines nine categories of disability: mental retardation, physical disability, emotional disturbance, visual impairment, hearing impairment, language disorders, learning disabilities, children with health problems, and children with chronic illnesses. The Ministry of Education and Science is responsible for the education of all children. The special school system in the Netherlands is well resourced and financed, and has a reputation for quality, so parents have little reason to look for alternative provision. Yet it is clear that there is a high percentage of children in special schools, possibly the highest in Europe.

In Germany all children, without exception, are educated from 6 to 18 years. Approximately 3.1 per cent of school children are enrolled in special education provision. The general policy is to enable all children and young people with disabilities to receive optimum education and training in relation to their needs, so that they can live an active and independent life in society. There is a general policy too of encouraging integration which provides the most appropriate education for the pupil in either mainstream or special school, to prepare them as well as possible for adult life. The legislation for disabled pupils in Germany covers education in general. The school laws are under the authority of the federal states (the *Länder*) and differ from state to state. The general legislation refers to seven categories of disability: mental retardation, physical disability, emotional disturbance, visual impairment, hearing impairment, language disorders and learning disabilities. All education provision is the responsibility of the Ministries of Education and Cultural Affairs.

In the Netherlands and Germany we witness a centralized and a decentralized system, which makes comparison difficult. It may be easier to compare the UK and Germany because of their similar administrative policies up to the early part of this decade; however, in the constantly changing scenario, the UK has to cope with recent changes brought about by the Education Reform Act of 1988, and its effect on pupils with SEN, while Germany during the same period is coping with the federal acquisition of the former East Germany, which has led to difficulties in classifying pupils with SEN and providing the necessary support. The authorities are attempting to develop a more flexible system of administration, resourcing and professional development in the new, larger German state.

This review of special educational systems in Europe shows that there is a general divergence of national practice in the use of categorization and placement of children with SEN. Those countries with an established tradition of special schooling, especially high-quality and well developed separate special provision as in the Netherlands, still retain the categorization of disability which matches the special school system and provides discrete provision for children within each school category. It can also be observed that certain European countries, particularly the Scandinavian countries, deliberately reject the notion of the categorization of pupils because it is perceived as a form of restrictive practice which reinforces notions of disability and stigma. Their national preference is for integrative or inclusive schooling, which is seen as a deliberate statement of human rights. Inclusive schooling in Scandinavian countries has come about as a result of parental pressure, based on the belief that in releasing the child from segregated education, and from the consequent development of a 'special' or 'disabled' identity, a mainstream education will provide a normal identity in a normal school which provides equal opportunities for all its pupils.

Much of the present situation in some European countries where segregated education is practised must also be directly linked to the positivist tradition associated with assessment built up in Europe since the establishment of the notion of intelligence quotients in the early part of the twentieth century. A system of categorization with rigid boundaries gives a rationale for the placement of children who challenge the education system, which is built around the notions of normality/abnormality and ability/disability. It follows logically that one can legislate for children who do not fit the 'norm' or who can be categorized as disabled. The legislation allows for policy and administration to proceed in a secure and concrete framework.

To reject categorization in favour of an alternative framework of, for example, the inclusion of all pupils in mainstream schools, leads to the redundancy of medical categorization, and brings in the concept of individual needs. An emphasis on individual needs raises issues related to professional responsibilities and the ethics of practice. This alternative position – operating without categorization – has no easily recognized reference points for the assessment of pupils; it becomes unclear what the terms 'ability' and 'normality' mean. Changing to an approach which prioritizes individual needs would make the education system more open and flexible and its access more difficult to manage; such open education systems are also notoriously difficult to control politically. For the legislator an inclusive system is hard to define in terms of access. Legislation throughout Europe guards against total inclusion on the grounds of the 'best interest' of the children concerned. Professionals too find it difficult to define the boundaries of their special role in an open school system.

All countries in Europe except for Italy operate a parallel education system of mainstream and special schools. Decisions about the placement of children, based in a parallel system on categories of handicap, are clear-cut and related to the criteria specified in legislation and policy documents. However, in a new alternative mainstreaming system decisions about children become more problematic and ambiguous. Accountability is focused on the individual professionals operating in the system; decisions and activities become personalized. In a tightly structured and administered system professional accountability is provided for in a more anonymous context. Responsibilities are not personalized because decisions about pupils are based on clear-cut categories, and therefore blame is deflected from individual professionals when decisions on the placement and treatment of pupils are challenged. It appears that in Europe special schooling functions best within clear boundaries, and the deliberate destruction of these boundaries inevitably leads to provision within a single mainstream system, which breaks down the criteria that made it necessary to have segregated schooling in the first place.

What we witness in Europe today are national traditions reflecting the need for security based on a categorization system which arose from a positivist tradition. Inclusive education brings an alternative, involving taking risks by moving away from safe segregated schooling in the belief that this is what meets the interest of the child. The countries of Europe which are leading the way are moving forward with the conviction that flexibility, with all its problems in creating quality of education for each individual, is in the best interests of the child, and ultimately of the citizens of the country. Each country is building its own value system in its schooling practices. Yet integration – the inclusion of all pupils, desegregation or schooling for the community – is the new moral imperative for all European countries.

Professional arguments inevitably centre around the defence of practices in special education for the purpose of increased and increasing integration. Most of the publicity material produced by national government, to be politically correct, must include the term 'integration' regardless of the reality of the practice. An illustration of this is the recent publication of the Directorate for Special Education in the Greek Ministry of National Education (Nicodemus, 1992, p. 160). The publication refers to the present situation in Greece thus: 'The Ministry's educational policy and philosophy concerning the education of children and youth with special needs is *clearly integration oriented* [emphasis in original], not only in theory but also in practice.'

There are no specific statistics in Greece concerning the number of children with SEN, but the international notion of 10 per cent of the population is accepted; therefore it is calculated that 180,000 children of school age are likely to have SEN. However, the total number of children and youth involved in special education programmes of the Ministry of Education in Greece is approximately 12,500, with 1200 teachers and 200 supporting service personnel. It appears that 0.07 per cent of children are being specially educated by the Greek Ministry of Education, while other pupils may be educated in private special schools or are in mainstream schools with little support or help. There are only 185 special schools in Greece for different categories of children with special needs, for example the hearing impaired, partially sighted, mentally retarded, socially maladjusted and autistic. There are also approximately 500 special classes or resource rooms in ordinary schools where children attend on a part-time basis, usually for one hour per day. This inadequate support system for a large and relatively unknown number of pupils, it is claimed, is a major trend in Greece today and is seen as a good and fruitful way towards school and social integration. There is a danger in the proposition of such a model of integration, with little quality of support in the mainstream school, being used as a model of inclusion. It is clear that in Greece there is a great need to develop country-wide support services for schools and pupils with SEN. The official document belies the true situation in its concluding paragraph:

> The field of special education in Greece is indeed under development. Much more must be done in the near future. The philosophy and practice of integration is widely accepted by the educational system and by the broad society. We are working step by step towards this direction. A basic strategy is to change the attitude and thinking of teachers and parents towards children with special needs. This change is the key point of all the actions and efforts in favour of the disabled. The whole school approach, and beyond this, the whole society approach to such problems guarantee ... better solutions. Some good practices are in function today and they may help us for the future relative planning.
> (Nicodemus, 1992, p. 160)

Does this conclusion suggest that the problem is not in the passing of enabling legislation which will ensure resources and policy, but that it is the attitudes of teachers and parents which are preventing this ideal from being achieved? Bardis (1993) clearly states that children with special needs in Athens and other large urban areas have some educational provision, but in rural areas of Greece there is a chronic lack of any quality of education for many pupils with SEN. Simply transporting certain children with disabilities to the local mainstream schools poses insurmountable problems in some areas. In Thessaly, for example, with a population of 700,000, only 130 students with special needs are receiving special services. One must be careful to read the official documentation offered in different countries and to investigate how it is exactly that they define pupils within the special education sector, and how precisely they provide education within that sector, or in the mainstream. Sending pupils to ordinary or mainstream schools with little or no support may be claimed as an educational practice for integration, yet in reality it may mask the lack of general provision in the mainstream or elsewhere.

One is forced to ask the question, how much are national perspectives a contingency response to the structural difficulties of implementing the best policies for children with special needs, or developing policies for integration? It is claimed, for example, that Italy embraced a radical policy of school integration because separate special education was not well developed (Daunt, 1991). But Booth (1982) claims that the radical transformation brought about by the National Act of 1971, which reversed the trend to provide for disabled children in special schools and classes, was the result of a social and political movement for all deviant and vulnerable groups in Italy. It may appear to many economically struggling countries in Europe that it is expedient to cut back on spending money on costly special schooling and to decide instead to develop integrational policies as a form of cost cutting.

Nevertheless, in Italy as early as 1971 school integration was established as a right for all children with SEN. In 1975 the Ministry of Education stated that the severity of the disablement, whether mental or physical, was not to limit integration in a mainstream class as long as admission was possible and positive for the disabled child. There may be historical parallels between this and the present situation in Greece. The Italian education authorities were accused of irresponsibility after disabled children had been brought out of institutions and special schools into mainstream classes (Ferro, 1981). Daunt (1991, p. 123) also refers to the dropping of quality of education for the sake of radical change. He states that 'it may be that standards were not always well guarded in these early days, later to be known as the period of "integrazione selvaggia" (wild integration) ... the provision for supporting personnel was irregular'.

However, in time the Italian system for integration became organized and manageable. Class sizes were reduced and regulated. Support teachers and ancillary helpers were provided, and mainstream teachers learned to accept their new clientele and to find means of teaching and resources appropriate to their needs. Italy moved totally and wholeheartedly towards an unidimensional, flexible and individualized educational framework. The decision was made to build up a supportive single education system rather than to develop a less adequate parallel and separate special school system.

SPAIN AND THE CONCEPT OF SPECIAL EDUCATIONAL NEEDS

Yet another country which has shown remarkable ability to transform its policy and practice in a short time is Spain. Spain provides compulsory education for children for ten years. The spread of the new model of integration in the Spanish special education system has been rapid and enthusiastic. The whole of school life is being altered by the acceptance of the principle of school integration, which has changed both the concept and design of educational services and educational practice. In Spain, as in the UK, there is acceptance of the new terminology of 'children with special educational needs' rather than children with disabilities or handicaps. This concept is linked to certain kinds of pedagogic help or services required to achieve the educational aims: that is, an educational need is described in terms of what is essential for the pupil to achieve certain educational objectives. Educational needs are now seen to be continuous, requiring action and resources, and include both temporary and permanent help and services. The Spanish concept now does not take into account the categorization of people according to available resources, but the conditions which affect the personal development of pupils and which justify the provision of particular help or services. The concept emphasizes the responsibility of the school in optimizing pupils' development. The SEN of a student are seen to be identified in relation to the school context, from which a solution to learning difficulties can be found.

In 1985, after the Royal Decree for children with SEN, the Ministry of Education and Science produced an integration plan to make it possible for children with special needs to be educated in mainstream schools. Since that time Spain has made remarkable progress in the administration, management and organization of the integration plan. The plan is developed by the establishment of whole schools as 'units': these are primary schools with at least eight classes and a pre-primary class. A maximum of 25 children are to be included in the first year of school, with a reduction in class numbers to this level year by year after the first year. Two support teachers are added to the existing school staff. Initially there were drawbacks to the programme because of the teachers' limited training, lack of school resources and the apprehension of parents and the public. However, two aims were devised:

–   to adopt whatever means are necessary to establish the credibility of the pro-
     gramme in the medium term;
–   to begin with volunteer schools to start the integration plan.

Teams were built up for early intervention and support. Provision of educational psychologists and support teachers was expanded, and a national resource centre for the development of the curriculum and teacher training was founded (Marchesi *et al.*, 1991).

The proposal was that the integration project would last for eight years and that there would be one integrated school for every 100–150,000 inhabitants each year, resulting in 50 per cent of all primary schools at the end of the eight-year period. At the same time an evaluation programme was undertaken with the aim of understanding and monitoring the development of the project. Quantitative and qualitative measures were used in a three-year longitudinal design. The results of the evaluation show that the project is fulfilling the education aims which were proposed. Changes, which are viewed as positive, have been made to overall planning in schools, to practical teaching and to the development of pupils' capabilities. The conclusions of the evaluation point to specific conditions, related to school staff, that enable the integration plan to work are:

•   agreement on the concept of teaching and the cohesion of the teaching team;
•   flexibility and efficiency in the management and organization of the school;
•   the willingness of teachers to receive training in order to undertake the educa-
     tional demands of integration;

- increased confidence and effectiveness of teachers as a result of further professional development.

For the pupils the success of integration had resulted in:

- social adaptation with classmates that might not have been found in segregated special schools;
- more cooperative and interactive behaviour with peers in the school;
- academic results of mainstream pupils remaining as expected for their age.

For the parents of the children studied it was also found that:

- attitudes towards integration were positive;
- attitudes were most positive from parents of children with serious educational difficulties.

Although at this stage the general integration plan involves children aged between 4 and 9, these pupils will continue in the mainstream schools, as far as possible, and will continue to challenge the schools' responses to their special and differential needs.

Spain has shown how responsive it has been to meeting the needs of 20 per cent of pupils who experience difficulties in school, and like the UK and France does not consider simply 2–6 per cent of pupils to have SEN, as was indicated earlier with reference to particular countries. What is happening in Spain has close parallels in the UK in terms of the use of terminology, the incorporation of integration into national legislation, and the establishment of a general ethos for the inclusion of all children in ordinary schools. As early as 1982 the Basque government in Spain designed a special education plan which proposed radical changes in the philosophy and structure of the special education services, as a result of which the following advances have been made (Eusko Jaurlaritza, 1989):

- Special classes have been set up in primary schools.
- Regional coordination centres for special education have been established.
- Resource centres for children with visual impairment have been opened.
- Specific teacher training programmes, comprising both initial training and continued professional development, have been undertaken for members of the multidisciplinary teams.
- Class size has been reduced where there are pupils with SEN.
- Support staff, such as classroom assistants and speech therapists, have been provided in ordinary schools.
- Guidelines on schools have been issued to enable parents to obtain the necessary information to help them to find integrative forms of schooling.
- More flexible financing arrangements have been made for special units.

In the Basque country a committee on special education was set up in 1987 and published a report in 1988 with a plan for improvements in the education system and guidelines for putting the improvements into practice. The report is based on five basic principles (O'Hanlon, 1993):

1. There should be the same educational aims for all pupils.
2. A policy of positive discrimination should operate for pupils with SEN.
3. SEN in children should be seen as relative, temporary, interactive, and linked to the curriculum.

4.   Integration should be an essential part of the education system.
5.   A change of attitudes must be developed in the aims and practice of schools, and in the community.

The changes that have taken place in such a short time in the Spanish education system and its radical redirection towards meeting the educational needs of all pupils in an open, flexible and integrated system are breathtaking. The strength of will and intention on the part of the educational establishment in providing the necessary support and resources for this reformation is also noteworthy. The integration plan is ambitious and far-reaching, and one hopes that the National Resource Centre for Special Education will give us a further record of this process of change and its long-term effects.

In conclusion, we observe in Europe a contrast in education systems, from highly technological systems to systems developing free and open education for pupils with SEN, which is revealed through the examination of practices of assessment, categorization and schooling. The highly technological systems exist in parts of Germany, the Netherlands, France, Luxembourg, Belgium, the Czech Republic, Hungary, Poland and Romania. However, in a general thematic sense, Germany, the Netherlands, France, Luxembourg and Belgium are heavily influenced by EU educational measures to bring about increased participation in ordinary schools for all pupils. There is a strong imperative for EU member states to evolve towards integration, which is witnessed by the *Resolution of the Council and the Ministers of Education of 31 May 1990* concerning the integration of children and young people with disabilities into ordinary systems of education (OJEC, 1990). The establishment of the RIF (Réseau d'Institutions de Formation) networks in 1990 by the ECYEB (European Community Youth Exchange Bureau), and other networks established through HELIOS and ERASMUS and funded by the EU, ensures the interaction of personnel in meetings, discussion, debate and action in the field of improving the educational opportunities for pupils with SEN throughout the EU. This influence is reaching beyond the formally affiliated EU countries to our eastern neighbours through projects such as TEMPUS.

The opening up of education systems to all pupils in Europe is viewed as a human rights issue, and countries such as Sweden, Denmark, Spain, some German *Länder* and some LEAs in the UK are leading the change from a highly technological system to a system which more easily responds to individual pupil needs by providing choice and valuing diversity. Although every educational system in Europe has its own problems in the organization and administration of policies for children with SEN, there are inherent difficulties in providing resources to develop practices that are not accepted and recognized within a particular culture and country. There are inevitable structural tensions in all educational systems which attempt to select and deselect pupils repeatedly on the basis of academic achievement. The most successful education systems in Europe in terms of aiming to produce a trained and professional workforce are not disadvantaged by their attempts to include SEN pupils in the process. More countries in Europe are finding out that special education in special schools and centres is expensive, helps only a limited number of children with SEN and does not bring about full participation and equality. Mainstream or ordinary schools are realizing that it is their responsibility to develop their teaching and curricula in order to cater for a greater diversity of pupils. In planning national educational strategies, treating children with

SEN in a separate context leads to problems of coordination and provision of services at a later stage. Many countries, in particular the Netherlands, are experiencing these difficulties and are trying to disentangle the complexity in formulating a new way forward. The traditions that have been established in the field of special education in Europe are in a state of transformation. The more firmly established educational systems and structures are proving more laborious to renew.

REFERENCES

Bardis, P. (1993) 'Integration of children with special needs in rural Greece'. In C. O'Hanlon (ed.) *Special Education: Integration in Europe*. London: David Fulton.

Booth, T. (1982) *National Perspectives, Special Needs Education*. Milton Keynes: Open University Press.

Bruce, M.G. (1991) 'In search of a European dimension in education'. *European Journal of Teacher Education*, **12**(3), 213–27.

Daunt, P. (1991) *Meeting Disability: a European Response*. London: Cassell.

DES (Department of Education and Science) (1978) *Special Educational Needs (The Warnock Report)*. London: HMSO.

Diniz, F.A. and Kropveld, P. (1982) *Teacher Training and Special Education in the Eighties*. Brussels: ATEE.

Diniz, F.A. and Kropveld, P. (1984) *The Preparation of Young People with Learning Difficulties for Adult Life*. Brussels: ATEE.

Diniz, F.A. and Kropveld, P. (1986) *Social Education and the Preparation of Young People with Learning Difficulties for Adult Life*. Brussels: ATEE.

Diniz, F.A. and Kropveld, P. (1987) *The Evaluation of Courses for the Training of Teachers in Special Education*. Brussels: ATEE.

Diniz, F.A. and Kropveld, P. (1989) *The Integration of Young People with Special Needs in Education*. Brussels: ATEE.

Drucker, P.F. (1989) *The New Realities*. London: Heinemann.

EASE (European Association for Special Education) (1990) *Information from EASE, vol. 11*, 1, 18.

Eusko Jaurlaritza (Ministry of Education) (1989) *Comprehensive and Integrative Schooling*. Spain: Basque Government.

Ferro, N. (1981) *The Education of the Handicapped Adolescent: the Integration of Handicapped Youth in Normal Schools in Italy*. Paris: OECD/CERI.

Heyning, J.R.C. and Kropveld, E.N. (1989) '*Limiting the Explosion*', Report on *Integration Revisited*. London: Thames Polytechnic and Brussels: ATEE.

Jørgensen, I.S. (1980) *Special Education in the European Community*. Brussels: Commission of the European Communities.

Marchesi, A., Gerardo, E., Elene, M., Mercedes, B. and Marisa, G. (1991) 'Assessment of the integration project in Spain'. *European Journal of Special Needs Education*, **6**(3), 185–9.

Mulcahy, D.G. (1991) 'In search of the European dimension in education'. *European Journal of Teacher Education*, **14**(3), 213–25.

Nicodemus, S. (1992) *Special Education in Greece*. Athens: Ministry of National Education and Religion.

O'Hanlon, C. (1993) *Special Education: Integration in Europe*. London: David Fulton.

OJEC (Official Journal of the European Communities) (1990) *Resolution of the Council and the Ministers of Education* meeting within the Council. Luxembourg: OJEC, C 162/2 of 3 July 1990.

Potts, P. (1982) *Origins (Special Needs in Education)*. Milton Keynes: Open University Press.

Rohrs, M. (1992) 'A united Europe as a challenge to education'. *European Journal of Intercultural Studies*, **3**, 59–70.

UNESCO (1988) *Review of the Present Situation of Special Education*. Paris: UNESCO.

Chapter 2

Inclusive Teacher Education in Europe: An Open Learning Approach

Patricia Potts

INTRODUCTION

I am going to discuss the value of and possibilities for an open learning approach to inclusive teacher education in Europe in the 1990s. By 'inclusive' I mean both mixed audiences for professional education and the development of generic curricula. By 'open learning' I mean access to courses that is not controlled by competitive entry requirements but which is shaped by student demand, so that study groups consist of people from a variety of backgrounds, with different perspectives on education, but who share a common current interest. Assessment is predominantly continuous and qualitative. Course materials are presented in a range of media and there is extensive student and tutor support. 'Open' learning is not the same as 'distance' learning. With advances in technology, with networks of local, regional, national and international study centres and with detailed, written feedback on all assignments, teaching and learning relationships in an open learning system can be closer than they often are in traditional 'face-to-face' institutions.

In this chapter I shall introduce what seem to me to be relevant European contexts for meeting the educational needs of people working with disabled students and those who experience difficulties in learning. I shall briefly outline the structure of the UK Open University and then describe in more detail the projects that my own group has been engaged in since 1979. Using this experience and information about the ways in which the UK Open University is already involved in Europe, I shall put forward some proposals for European collaboration. I shall conclude that an open, inclusive approach to teacher education is responsive to the educational requirements of both teachers and taught.

EUROPEAN CONTEXTS FOR TEACHER EDUCATION

The map of Europe has been transformed in the last four years. Developing an appropriate education system for learners of all abilities, interests and ages entails responding to the new, or rather the re-emergence of old, geographical boundaries. Open learning and teacher education are acknowledged priorities within the European Community.

The European Community and 'open distance learning'

European Community support for developing what it calls 'open distance learning' stems from a Resolution of the European Parliament of 10 July 1987, which asked for information on the feasibility of a European Open University. In November 1991 a memorandum entitled 'Open Distance Learning in the European Community' was presented to the Council of Ministers. The Commission recommended that existing networks should be used in preference to the establishment of a new institution and that the promotion of open distance learning should be an EC priority. The proposed strategy for open distance learning includes: the co-production of materials; the establishment of study centres; the creation of data banks; and the mutual recognition and accreditation of courses. The Secretariat of the European Association of Distance Teaching Universities (EADTU) argues that:

> The adoption of such a strategy should extend access to, and improve the quality of, vocational training throughout the Community. It should also enable participation in higher education to be extended, particularly in the context of continuing and recurrent education. Availability of higher quality distance learning materials and systems can strengthen institution-based education and training by extending its scope and enhancing of quality.
> (EADTU Secretariat, 1991)

The European Trade Union Committee for Education (ETUCE) and teacher education

A priority for ETUCE at the moment is teacher education. A Teacher Education Working Group (TEWG) has been set up, with a Danish chair and a British secretary and has reported (ETUCE, 1994) on the following issues: staff development; management of the curriculum; resources; career development; status; and mobility. Previous ETUCE working group reports have influenced EC policy and it is expected that the TEWG report will do the same.

Equal opportunities and 'values' education

As the countries of Eastern and Western Europe come closer together politically and there is pressure to increase the membership of the European Community, so there are increasing fears of a 'Fortress Europe' in which the new, extended fraternity will look inward and backward, refusing, for example, to recognize the rights of ethnic minorities, including the right to access to education. The tone of recent European initiatives on the education of disabled students and those who experience difficulties in learning is inclusive, supportive of greater integration. See, for example, a recent resolution of the EC Council and Ministers of Education (OJEC, 1990). However, this commitment exists alongside proposals for tighter controls on immigration, workers' rights and citizenship: processes of inclusion and exclusion operating simultaneously.

While there are inequalities of access to education across Europe, there is also an awareness that 'values' need to be an explicit part of the curriculum, both for school students and for teachers. The themes of the Association for Teacher Education in Europe (ATEE) 18th annual conference, held in September 1993 in Lisbon, were 'Teacher Training' and 'Values Education'. The topics for the 15 working groups covered:

- technology and communication;
- initial and in-service teacher education;
- curricular issues (early years, science, language, vocational);
- innovation and management issues;
- equal opportunities (intercultural education, gender, human rights and peace education);
- special education.

Looking at the list, I wondered why special education had been separated out from the discussions of curriculum development, equal opportunities, or technology and communication. A child's cultural community, home language, gender and economic status are all factors that affect his or her capacity to benefit from the education on offer, as well as, in some places, affecting the provision itself.

Approaches to special education

How shall a curriculum for teacher education be designed? This depends on what is seen as the main task of a particular course, for this will determine both its content and its preferred audience. The task of preparing people to work with disabled students or with those who experience difficulties in learning is understood by different educators to involve very different elements. Different approaches reflect different value-systems.

For example, if the task is seen as one of producing people to work in a specialized system, in which children are selected for a particular educational setting according to their level of attainment or their requirements for particular equipment or therapy, then the curriculum for such a course will focus on the details of physical and sensory disability, the identification and assessment of individual deficits and the delivery of curricula for small, homogeneous groups of pupils. The audience for a specialized course will itself be small and homogeneous, reflecting the expected pattern of professional responsibility.

If, on the other hand, the task is seen as producing people to work in a system in which children will be taught in mixed-ability groupings in the mainstream, then the course will focus on school curriculum development and flexible learning support systems rather than on disability. Such a course would be generic and would set discussions of disability and difficulty in learning within the context of the education system as a whole. The audience for this kind of course will be large and diverse, reflecting the expectation of shared professional responsibilities.

The first kind of course supports a segregated system of special education and the second kind supports a process of integration. In practice, courses may contain elements of both approaches; this, although contradictory in terms of the underlying value-systems, reflects the situation that exists, certainly in the UK, in which both specialized and generic approaches are supported. Integration is officially seen to be desirable, but not possible, for all students.

From her study of special educational policy and provision across Europe, Christine O'Hanlon (1993) concludes that the process of integration is compatible with the education of a professional and skilled workforce, whereas a segregated system of special provision is expensive, helps only a small number of children and does not guarantee their subsequent participation in society. She also sees that special education is undergoing a transformation, as countries move to and fro between a selective and an inclusive approach. In the context of differences in educational policy and practice that have deep cultural and historical roots, can collaboration between countries build creatively on the present destabilization?

THE UNITED KINGDOM OPEN UNIVERSITY AND INCLUSIVE TEACHER EDUCATION

The UK Open University was set up in 1969, with the first courses being presented in 1971, to provide adults with the opportunity to study for a degree, to provide courses for professional development and to provide short courses and study packs for community education. The university now includes the Faculties of Arts, Mathematics, Science, Social Sciences and Technology, the Schools of Education and Management, the Department of Continuing Education and the OU/BBC production centre. There are about 74,000 undergraduate students, 6500 postgraduate students and 90,000 associate and continuing education students. These numbers include about 3000 disabled students each year. Students enrol on a first come, first served basis. Course materials are produced centrally but tutoring and counselling services are administered by the 13 regional offices. A full credit course, involving about 440 hours of study time, costs about £220; postgraduate courses, such as the School of Education's taught master's degree costs about £400 for each of the three modules. The study year runs from February to October.

Initial teacher education (ITE) at the Open University

In February 1994, 1000 students enrolled on the Open University School of Education's eighteen-month, part-time Postgraduate Certificate in Education (PGCE), with 500 following the primary course, focusing on early years or later years, and 500 following the secondary course in one of six subject areas: English, mathematics, science, technology, history, and French. Market research found that a large number of mature graduates were interested in becoming teachers, including a significant proportion whose background was in science and mathematics, core subjects of the UK National

Curriculum but in which there is an acute shortage of trained staff. The Department for Education (DfE) is funding the programme, which includes partnership arrangements with schools across the country who supervise the students' school-based work. In developing this 'mentoring' role, senior teachers will be supported by the central Open University course team and work closely with the students' Open University tutors. Assessment will be through a folio of work and self-assessment. It is hoped that the Open University PGCE model will facilitate continuity between ITE and in-service education.

The OU/PGCE course is divided into seven study blocks, grouped into three stages with each stage involving a period of full-time school placement, from three weeks in stage 1 to eight weeks in stage 3. Apart from issues such as curriculum planning, classroom management and assessment related to students' particular interests, there are five themes running through the course:

1   the relation of competence, experience and knowledge to developing the teaching role;
2   the significance of language for learning;
3   the promotion of equal opportunities through the teaching role;
4   an understanding of how school policies can create the conditions for successful and effective institutions;
5   information technology.

These themes are also the subject of block 5, in stage 3 of the course, when students spend 30 hours on each of the following units: Language and Learning; Learning for All; and Effective Schools.

The Open University Special Education Group

I joined the then Faculty of Education in 1979. There were three of us in the special education group and our first course, 'Special Needs in Education' (E241), was presented to 1500 undergraduate and associate students in 1982. This was a half-credit course consisting of 16 units of text, eight television programmes, four double-sided audio cassettes and two specially commissioned and edited readers. Tutor groups consisted of up to 30 students, who completed five assignments and one examination during the course.

In 1986 we produced a multi-media in-service education resource pack, entitled 'Teaching for Diversity: Preventing Difficulties in Learning' (EP538), designed for school-based groups working without an Open University tutor. The course consisted of a study guide with activities for 19 two-hour sessions, a reader and a video cassette with eight 10- to 15-minute sequences.

In 1987 our project-based postgraduate course 'Applied Studies in Difficulties in Learning in Education' (E806) was presented to about 450 students. Their project work was supported by a project guide and a series of three new readers. Students were in smaller tutor groups and enjoyed more tutor-contact hours than was the standard for undergraduate courses. E806 forms the second half of our Advanced Diploma in 'Special Needs in Education' (D06).

In 1992 our second undergraduate course 'Learning for All' (E242) was presented to about 950 students and our first master's degree module 'Developing Inclusive Curricula: Equality and Diversity in Education' (E829) will be presented in 1995.

Over the years we have developed a shared approach to the discussion of the issues which face disabled learners and those who experience difficulties in learning or other kinds of difficulties. Here is an extract from the introduction to the 'Learning for All' course guide (Open University, 1992):

> 'Learning for All' is a course for anyone with an interest in the education of children and young people who experience difficulties in learning in nurseries, schools or colleges or who have disabilities. The course is about difficulties in learning and the practices and policies which can help to overcome them. It is concerned with all children and young people who may experience difficulties, whatever their level of attainment; those who become disaffected, or are provided with an inappropriate or unstimulating curriculum; those who, with the assistance of technology, can gain access to a higher degree and those who never fully develop communication through language. 'Learning for All' covers the age range from pre-school to further and higher education, although there is an emphasis on the years of compulsory schooling. ...
>
> Difficulties in learning can arise in any aspect of the curriculum and are hence the responsibility of all teachers. The course is as much about teaching science, drama or poetry to a diversity of students, so that all of them can engage in a broad curriculum, as it is about the acquisition of literacy and numeracy. It explores the extent to which specialist knowledge and skills are required to overcome difficulties and the precise nature of such expertise; for example, sign language for working with children and young people who are deaf, physiotherapy and 'conductive education' techniques for cerebral palsy. However, there is an emphasis on the knowledge required to work with individual students rather than categorized groups.
>
> 'Learning for All' is an introductory course and assumes no previous knowledge of other education courses. It does assume that all its students bring their own particular experiences of the education system and that these provide them with an important source of ideas about the way difficulties in learning can be created and resolved. We try to avoid the use of jargon and urge our students to do the same. We ask them to assess critically what they read, including what we ourselves write, rather than to follow an 'official' version of the truth about learning.

THE UK OPEN UNIVERSITY IN EUROPE

It is now possible for anyone resident in the member states of the European Union to register as a student with the UK Open University (UKOU) and nearly all of the OU's courses are available. The number of OU students resident outside the UK is expected to be about 10,000 by the year 2000. Depending on the numbers of students and the courses they choose, it is likely that local tutors will be employed for some of the groups based in Europe and the UKOU may hold residential summer schools on the continent.

The UK Open University has coordinators in a number of European cities, including Brussels, the Hague, Frankfurt, Paris, Milan, Geneva and Vienna, who answer enquiries, channel applications and organize publicity. The system began in the mid-1980s, funded from the UK. Students living on the continent of Europe are attached to a UKOU regional office, originally Newcastle for the Benelux countries and Cambridge for the rest of the EU, though Newcastle is about to assume complete responsibility. European students are supported in the same way as domestic students by the School of Education staff tutors in these two regions and costs come out of their regional budgets. If adequate funding can be put together, it is possible that a European region of the UKOU may be established, probably in Brussels. The UKOU is an active member of European associations for distance learning, for example SATURN, which is based in Amsterdam, and it is likely that these contacts will result in regular staff exchanges.

Management in the European marketplace

The UKOU department which has the most extensive links is the School of Management, for whom Europe is becoming an increasingly important market. As the School is funded solely by means of fee income and does not receive British taxpayers' money, it can charge students the same fee right across Europe. Other faculties, which are publicly funded, have to charge overseas students an additional £150. However, the School of Management courses are more expensive than those presented by other departments. Also, charging the same fee across Europe is not equitable, as this might be cheap for some students and very dear for others. Similarly, tutors are paid the same across Europe, which would be good money where student fees seem expensive and a poor reward where student fees seem low. Course team members wish to resolve these inequalities.

The 'institution-as-tutor model' and collaboration in Eastern Europe

UKOU courses are usually presented and taught on the continent in English. However, the School of Management has secured funding from two new funding programmes, the EU TEMPUS programme and the British government 'Know-how' fund, to develop an initiative in Eastern Europe which involves the translation of OU materials.

The UKOU was approached in 1989 by members of the 'Budapest Platform' group who were interested both in management training and distance learning. A contractual arrangement was agreed between the UKOU and Eurocontact, a company set up by the Hungarians and administered, initially, by a professor and a group of postgraduates at Budapest University. Students are registered with the company and with the UKOU; their fee goes to the company and the OU receives a commission.

The scheme has evolved in the following way:

–   Twenty students enrolled on the UKOU foundation course, 'The Effective Manager', which they studied in English. The aim was that they would, in turn, become tutors for subsequent groups of students and that they would undertake the translation of the materials into Hungarian.
–   The students received tutor training, which covered areas such as counselling and the marking of assignments.
–   The translation of the English materials was verified by a former UKOU editor and printed locally.
–   The students took an examination set by the UKOU course team, but their results were moderated by a Hungarian examination board, which included a member of the UKOU parent examination board.

A further stage would be the preparation of open learning materials by local course teams. The UKOU's Institute of Educational Technology (IET) runs a month's course annually for overseas participants on the writing of open learning materials.

Communication systems across Europe

The Academic Computing Services (ACS) department of the UKOU is centrally involved in the operation and extension of international data networks and conferences and E-mail systems, for academics, for teachers and schools, and for open learning students. For example, GEONET is a European consortium which aims to develop dial-up access, facilitating a much wider use of networks, which have, on the continent, mainly been accessible to those who are on-site at universities. Remote students can use the network at local telephone rates. OU students based on the continent can link up with people in the UK using the COSY system. The OU's Disabled Students' Office and Institute of Educational Technology collaborate with ACS to develop communication systems of particular relevance to the requirements of disabled students. Technology is rapidly reducing the distance between learners.

OPEN LEARNING NETWORKS FOR THE 1990s

What kinds of structure and project can therefore promote open learning across Europe and what would be their aims? Here are some proposals:

- to develop a Euro-Regional Office for the coordination of open learning networks;
- to develop contractual partnerships between the UKOU and institutions in other European countries for the translation of UKOU course material for local users;
- to set up international course teams for the co-production of courses. UKOU course teams work together for two to three years, depending on the specific nature of the course. Team membership is usually the major, but not the sole, commitment of members. UKOU course teams include the following range of personnel: authors, course manager, editor/s, secretary, television/audio producer/s, designer, librarian and external assessor;
- to develop systems for evaluating and accrediting courses and for the transfer of credit from one course to another. The UKOU already has a credit transfer arrangement with the Dutch Open University;
- to develop course materials of relevance to the education of disabled people and those who experience difficulties in learning. These could take the form of the OU/PGCE course for initial training, a modular pack for in-service education or the sequential form of an advanced diploma at postgraduate level, which would require students to follow a generic core course and then pursue their particular interests in more detail by means of small-scale research projects;
- to design materials, assignments and assessment strategies that are accessible to disabled people so that their opportunities for educational and professional development are extended.

CONCLUSIONS: AN OPEN LEARNING APPROACH TO INCLUSIVE TEACHER EDUCATION

I have discussed the work of my group at the UKOU in the context of political and educational developments in Europe. Opportunities for collaboration are multiplying, despite the existing range of perspectives on special education, and I have made some suggestions for specific projects. I have argued for an inclusive, rather than an exclusive and specialized, approach to the education of disabled students and those who experience difficulties in learning. I have also argued that this should be reflected in the approach to the education of their teachers.

Meeting the educational needs of all children and young people should be a theme for all professional curricula, not the special focus of a few. The variety of formats, the flexibility of content and possible assessment strategies and the extensive networks of support for open learning students provide a model for developing teachers' own practice. An open, inclusive approach to teacher education is responsive to the educational requirements of both teachers and taught.

REFERENCES

EADTU Secretariat (European Association of Distance Learning Universities) (1991) 'The EC defines its priorities for education and training in the nineties'. *EADTU News*, **9**, 7–9.

ETUCE (European Teacher Trade Union Committee for Education) (1994) *Teacher Education in Europe*. Brussels: ETUCE.

O'Hanlon, C. (1993) 'The European dimension in integration and special needs education'. *Research Papers in Education: Policy and Practice*, **8**(1), 19–32.

OJEC (Official Journal of the European Communities) (1990) *Resolution of the Council and the Ministers of Education meeting within the Council, C16222/2*. Brussels: European Communities.

Open University (1992) 'Learning for All' (E242). Milton Keynes: Open University.

Chapter 3

Best Practices Criteria in Inclusive Education: A Basis of Teacher Education

David Mitchell

INTRODUCTION

In this chapter I shall present a model for preparing staff to work with students with special educational needs in secondary schools. The model is based on a scale for designing and evaluating secondary school programmes for students with special needs (Mitchell, 1988; Mitchell, 1993; Mitchell *et al.*, 1991). The scale represents one of the major outcomes from Project One in Seven, a New Zealand research project that focused on the 14 to 15 per cent (i.e. 'one in seven') of secondary school students who might be expected to have special educational needs requiring adaptation of curricula and teaching in the context of inclusive education. The chapter will first outline key definitions, then describe Project One in Seven and how the 41 items making up the scale were developed, and finally summarize the implications of the scale for preparing teachers to work with students with special needs in secondary schools.

DEFINITIONS

For the purposes of this chapter, two terms need to be defined; their definitions are taken from the final report of the UNESCO Regional Seminar on Policy, Planning and Organization of Education for Children and Young People with Special Needs, which was held in Harbin, China 1–4 February 1993 and to which I was a UNESCO consultant.

Special educational needs are deemed to be those which arise from disabilities or learning difficulties or from special abilities (i.e. gifted and talented students). It is important to recognize that children with special educational needs may have other special needs. For example, children with special educational needs resulting from deafness may also come from an ethnic minority group or from socially disadvantaged families, or they may be nomadic or travellers' children.

Inclusive schools have a philosophy of providing education for all children. They recognize and respond to the diversity of their schools' populations. They accommodate to children's different styles and rates of learning. Inclusive schools ensure equality of education through appropriate curriculum, school organization, use of resources and partnerships with their communities.

PROJECT ONE IN SEVEN

The overall aim of Project One in Seven was to assist secondary schools to improve the quality of their programmes for students with special educational needs. The project culminated in the development of 41 criteria contained in a scale designed to evaluate how secondary schools accommodate their policies and programmes to students with special needs and assist them to make appropriate improvements.

The methodology of Project One in Seven required the work covered in the project to fall into two phases. In phase 1, studies were carried out of seven New Zealand secondary schools in order not only to develop interview procedures and to test out ways of writing whole-school case studies, but also to obtain substantive information bearing on the issues being investigated. In phase 2 the concern was with developing intervention strategies to assist secondary schools to critically evaluate and improve the quality of their work with students with special educational needs.

The following features characterized the approach employed in phase 1:

1. The methodology drew heavily upon ethnographic approaches in an attempt to elucidate how the participants in the seven secondary schools conceptualized their own attitudes and behaviour in relation to students with special educational needs.
2. The project focused on how individual schools as social systems adapt to students with special educational needs. In this 'whole-school' approach, attempts were made to relate the individual participants' behaviours and beliefs to the ethos or culture of the school.
3. The principal sources of data were interviews conducted with participants in the schools, the resulting case studies relying heavily upon the constructs and actual words employed by the participants.
4. Data went through a cyclic process of gradual refinement, with attempts to clarify the views of individual respondents before drawing these together into a description of the whole school and, ultimately, looking for patterns across all of the schools in the study.
5. In order to minimize the possibility of distorting data, care was taken to triangulate information, either by means of cross-checking among the various respondents or by comparing oral and written information. Participants were asked, too, to verify both the 'raw data' they provided in the interviews and, later, how their information and comments were incorporated in the case study report on their school. Finally, at each stage of the analysis, 'audit trails' were carefully established, so that it is possible to readily retrieve the sources for any generalization that is made in the report. The major outcome of this phase of the study was the development of a first draft of a set of 'best practice' criteria for secondary school programmes for students with special educational needs.

The second phase built on the results of phase 1 and included the following steps:

1. Interviews were held with groups of teachers and parents in Wales (one location) and New Zealand (four locations) to refine the best practice criteria developed in phase 1.
2. Field trials were held in four New Zealand schools to further refine the criteria, particularly with respect to their face validity and ease of use in actual school settings.
3. Further discussions were held with groups of teachers and school administrators in the United Kingdom, the United States and New Zealand, from which emerged a set of 'best practices' criteria in working with students who are disabled or who have special abilities. These criteria were further tested in field trials held in four other New Zealand secondary schools and in discussions with groups of secondary school teachers and administrators in New Zealand, the United Kingdom and the United States.

As a result of the above procedures, a 41-item scale for evaluating secondary school policies and programmes for students with special educational needs was developed. The items fall into the following eight broad groups:

- school policy (8 items);
- Identification and assessment (5 items);
- curriculum and programme delivery (7 items);
- school organization (6 items);
- physical adaptations (3 items);
- teacher education and induction (3 items);
- respect for students with special educational needs (4 items);
- relationships with external agencies and other schools (5 items);

Two examples of these criteria, together with questions for staff, parents and students that are designed to elicit information to the criteria, are as follows:

Criterion #7: The school's procedures for reviewing policies and practices for students with special educational needs include consulting with staff members, sampling the views of families and students, and drawing upon the opinions of external consultants.

Questions: all staff

7.1 When the school's policies and practices are reviewed, are the views of students with special educational needs and their families sought?
7.2 Are opinions of external consultants sought?

Question: students

7.3 Have the teachers ever asked you about what you think of the school?

Question: parents

7.4 Has the school ever asked you what you think about how it is catering for students with special educational needs?

Criterion #12: As with all students, records relating to individual students with special educational needs are handled with sensitivity to the rights of students and their families to have private information treated with the maximum degree of confidentiality.

Questions: all staff

12.1   Under what conditions do you have access to student records?
12.2   Under what conditions do parents have access to student records?
12.3   Under what conditions do students have access to their own records?
12.4   Under what conditions do other agencies have access to student records?

Question: students

12.5   Many students have files of information about their school work and doctor's report, etc. Who is allowed to see these files?

Probes

Are your parents allowed to see them?
Are you allowed to see them?

Questions: parents

12.6   Do you have access to your child's records?
12.7   Who does have access to your child's records?
12.8   Do you think that your child should have access to his or her records?
12.9   Should your permission be sought before people outside the school are allowed to see your child's records?

The scale is intended to be used in the programme evaluation procedures that are (1) *conjoint* (i.e. carried out jointly by members of the school and outside evaluators); (2) *formative* (i.e. intended to bring about changes in the school in order to better meet the criteria); and (3) oriented to *process* as well as to outcome (i.e. concerned with the policies and methods, as well as the accomplishments).

Seven core values underpin the scale. In the remainder of this section these values will be described, one or two illustrative items from the scale will be cited for each one, and the implications for the pre-service training and in-service development of teachers in regular classrooms will be indicated.

Value 1 – The right to education: the school recognizes and asserts that persons with special educational needs have the right to an education that will help them develop to their potential.

Criterion #2: The school has a policy that all students with special educational needs are accepted as having full rights of access to all the educational resources and programmes provided to and by the school and this policy is clearly expressed in written materials that are readily available to staff, parents or caregivers and students.

Aims of pre-service teacher education

- to be aware of the key literature on the rights of persons with disabilities, normalization, integrated education, inclusive schools, and mainstreaming;
- to be aware of relevant legislation and its interpretation;
- to act as advocates on behalf of students with special educational needs;
- to identify factors which present barriers to students with special educational needs having full access to the schools and their programmes;
- to develop strategies for ensuring improved access to schools and their programmes.

Aims of in-service staff development

- as for pre-service teacher education, but with a focus on the participants' individual schools;
- To develop written policies for participants' schools in accord with the above criterion.

Value 2 – Respect for students with special educational needs: the school enhances the self-esteem of students with special educational needs.

Criterion #36: Students with special educational needs and/or their advocates have a voice to the fullest extent possible in their own provision and feel that they are receiving an appropriate education.

Aims of pre-service teacher education

- to be aware of the range of attitudes held towards students with special educational needs;
- to develop ways of combating negative or harmful attitudes and of developing positive ways of interacting with such students. These may be through such means as self-examination, modelling, use of 'buddies', and the distribution of appropriate information on special educational needs;
- to be aware of the need to consult with students with special educational needs and their parents or caregivers on provisions to be made for these students;
- to develop skills in interacting with students with special educational needs and their parents or caregivers in ways that are respectful of their needs and rights;
- to use appropriate language when referring to students with special educational needs and to take responsibility for correcting other people's language when it is demeaning of students with special educational needs.

Aims of in-service staff development

- As for pre-service teacher education, but with the focus on students for whom the individual participants have some responsibility;
- to analyse individual schools' 'cultures' with respect to the attitudes towards individual differences.

Value 3 – Community coherence: the school enhances the social coherence and solidarity of the community by recognizing and asserting that students with special educational needs have the right to be educated in inclusive settings and to be full and effective participants in their communities.

Criterion #26: Students with special educational needs receive their schooling with their peers and are withdrawn from their classes only in exceptional circumstances when their needs cannot be adequately met in regular classes even with the help of resource teachers.

Aims of pre-service teacher education

- to accept responsibility to teach to the diverse needs within the classroom;
- to recognize the importance of adopting a 'whole-school' approach to students with special educational needs.

Aims of in-service staff development

- As for pre-service teacher education, but with a focus on participants' individual schools.

Value 4 – Sensitivity to the diversity among students: the school is sensitive to and supportive of the needs arising from differences in its students' backgrounds and ensures that its goals and processes are culturally and ecologically valid.

Criterion #14: Programmes for students with special educational needs are sensitive to background variables, especially ethnicity, gender, socioeconomic status, and geographical location.

Aims of pre-service teacher education

- to be aware that special educational needs interact with other background variables which may have the effect of compounding the primary difficulty.

Aims of in-service staff development

- as for pre-service teacher education, but with a focus on participants' individual schools.

Value 5 – Family integrity: the programme strengthens the family by respecting its integrity, by enhancing the competence of its members, by helping its members to access resources appropriate to the needs of persons with disabilities, and by recognizing its uniqueness.

Criterion #17: There is an active policy of involving the family of a student when deciding upon provisions for students with special educational needs.

Aims of pre-service teacher education

- to have first-hand contact with parents or caregivers of students with special educational needs;

- to be aware of how parents and caregivers are actively involved in developing individual education plans for their child with special educational needs.

Aims of in-service staff development

- as for pre-service teacher education, but with a focus on students for whom the individual teacher has some responsibility.

Value 6 – Professional standards: the schools seek to achieve the highest professional standards in the design and implementation of their work. Theory and research are integrated in the assessment of students with special educational needs, in the design of curriculum, and in the selection of appropriate teaching methods.

Criterion #10: The school has a flexible procedure for evaluating educational achievement that ensures valid assessment of students with special educational needs and their learning environments and which leads to action to improve such students' learning and quality of life.

Aims of pre-service teacher education

- to be skilled in designing and interpreting curriculum-based and criterion-referenced assessment procedures;
- to understand what is meant by 'ecological assessment';
- to be aware of the strengths and weaknesses of standardized assessment procedures;
- To design learning tasks based on information from a range of assessment data.

Aims of in-service staff development

- as for pre-service teacher education, but with the focus on students for whom the individual teacher has some responsibility.

Criterion #18: Each department in the school has developed techniques for adapting its curriculum and teaching so that they are accessible, rewarding and challenging to the skills and learning styles of students with special educational needs.

Aims of the pre-service teacher education

- to be able to recognize the range of special educational needs of students for whom individual educational programmes have not been developed;
- to develop teaching strategies that are sufficiently flexible to accommodate to the range of special educational needs (e.g. setting of realistic expectations for achievement, group work, cooperative teaching, graduated exercises, appropriate pacing, appropriate classroom management techniques, peer tutoring, an appropriate mix of abstract and practical examples, recognition of different learning styles, and appropriate assessment criteria and methods);
- to put these skills into practice in teaching practice.

Aims of in-service staff development

- as for pre-service teacher education, but with the focus on students for whom the individual teacher has some responsibility.

Value 7 – Accountability: the programme is accountable for the efficient and equitable management of its resources.

Criterion #6: The school continuously undertakes systematic reviews of its philosophies, policies and practices as they affect students with special education needs. In particular, it takes into account the impact on students with special educational needs of decisions made in such areas as school organization, the timetable, curriculum and the allocation of space, time and personnel resources.

Aims of pre-service teacher education

- to understand the principles and practices of whole-school reviews, including self- and conjoint evaluation procedures.

Aims of in-service staff development

- to participate in internally conducted whole-school reviews of programmes for students with special educational needs.

CONCLUSION

This chapter has outlined the development and application of a scale for evaluating secondary school programmes for students with special needs. The criteria employed in the scale resulted from extensive field trials in New Zealand, but also took account of some comment relating to secondary schools in the United Kingdom and the United States. The criteria were then used as a basis for suggesting a comprehensive pro-gramme for preparing personnel to work with students with special educational needs in secondary schools. The underlying philosophy of the programme was that a whole-school approach is necessary if students with special educational needs are to receive appropriate education within the context of being accepted as full members of a secondary school.

REFERENCES

Mitchell, D.R. (ed.) (1988) *One in Seven Final Report*. Hamilton: University of Waikato.
Mitchell. D. (1993) *Preparing Personnel for Working with Students with Special Educational Needs in Secondary Schools*. Paris: UNESCO.
Mitchell, D., Lowden, G. and Crouse, W. (1991) 'Designing and evaluating programmes for students with special educational needs in secondary school'. *Set* (New Zealand Council for Educational Research, Wellington, New Zealand).
UNESCO (1993) *Policy, Planning and Organisation for Children and Young People with Special Needs*. Report of a regional seminar, Harbin, 1–4 February. Paris: UNESCO.

Part II

Professional Development for Inclusive Education

Chapter 4

Managing Training for Special Educational Needs

Mel Johnson, Mike Wright and Garry Hornby

INTRODUCTION

The past 25 years have seen a range of changes in the ways in which local education authorities and schools in England and Wales have been required to respond to pupils with special educational needs. Systems of referral, assessment and identification have undergone a variety of adjustments as a result of the 1981 Education Act. Likewise LEA and school organization systems have been exposed to a rapid process of change in order to accommodate the requirements of the more recent Education Act 1988 with its profound implications for practice and provision (Smith, 1992). The implication of the National Curriculum, local management of schools (LMS) and the 1992 White Paper all bring management challenges to schools, not least because of the potential for conflict with the under-resourced 1981 Education Act. Alterations in in-service funding arrangements, that is grants for educational support and training (GEST), have also had considerable impact on training for teachers of children with SEN (Hodgson and Trotter, 1989; Visser, 1991).

These dramatic changes force managers into pragmatic solutions which are often in conflict with the more liberal philosophical aspirations which have guided recent developments in the SEN field. These philosophical trends have been developing throughout the early 1970s across the USA and Europe, but in England were finally distilled into realistic recommendations in the Warnock Report (DES, 1978). The recommendations of the Warnock Report fundamentally challenged the historical practice of dealing educationally with children with disabilities or learning difficulties in a segregated fashion. Children were deemed to have the right to be educated in their neighbourhood school, sharing learning with their peers. There was no longer to be a perceived separation between children with disabilities and their non-disabled peers. A continuum of provision was considered necessary to meet the continuum of needs (Hornby, 1992).

This philosophical aspiration raised significant management problems for LEAs, schools and those responsible for training courses at institutes of higher education. No longer was the teaching of the 'slow learner' to be in the exclusive hands of the specialist teacher. No longer did it seem proper to exclude such pupils from the mainstream curriculum experience and deal with skill deficits in isolation. No longer was it deemed appropriate to offer highly specialist training courses exclusively to the special needs teacher (Robson and Wright, 1989).

The message was clear: there was to be shared responsibility for SEN provision and practice, and a need was recognized for the development of a whole-school/LEA management strategy with ownership of the issues understood by everyone. At the LEA or school level there could be no place for special needs departments as the section taking sole responsibility for the least effective learners. SEN departments now have changed roles and functions, that is, they have become the advisory, support and strategic planners to assist all teachers to deliver the curriculum to all children (Dean, 1989; Roaf, 1991).

In order to offer flexible training opportunities for this much wider range of professionals, LEAs and institutions of higher education have had to develop partnerships and to become quite innovative in their course design, provision and practice. No longer is there a place for the 'hero innovator' course leader as the sole deliverer offering a theoretical rationale to teachers who aspire to achieve their master's ticket to promotion in the field of SEN.

> In many ways the situation of the courses and course tutor in the college was analogous to the position of special schools in the school system. The idea of special education expertise ensured that such courses were isolated from the mainstream, for few colleges could afford a range of 'experts'. Consequently the one expert was totally absorbed in running his/her course, and had only minimal and token inputs with the initial training courses. This token presence was then justified by the theory that all students should have experience of ordinary children before they retrained, via the in-service course, for the teaching of the handicapped. The myth of an expertise different in kind from that available to the ordinary school teacher was not only reinforced by the isolation of both training and school, but was often further strengthened by expertise based on the pathological view of learning difficulties. Not surprisingly many such courses became propagators of the myth of the Hero-Innovator, seeing their role as one of taking the gospel of Special Education treatment to a hostile and uncomprehending world.
>
> (Wright, 1989, p. 151)

Courses now need to be practically led by credible, experienced practitioners with all activity firmly rooted in classroom practice.

In this new context, a range of managers emerges: SEN coordinators, SEN governors, SEN consultants and subject specialists. The most important, of course, are the class teachers who have prime responsibility to manage colleagues, pupils, a range of resources, classroom space, the delivery of the curriculum, the process of assessment, recording and reporting, personal and professional development time, and finally time itself.

In order to meet the needs of these diverse groups, course options in in-service training (INSET) need to be flexible and accessible. Consideration has to be given to mode and place of delivery, range of choices, coherent pathways to accommodate specialisms, the validation of course content, and the credit value of prior learning. Possibilities for the mentorship of self-study units and distance learning packages need to be considered and managed. Although the management responsibilities for all of the professional workers have increased, it is considered that their needs can be embedded in a modularized training programme which offers a range of pathways and obvious choices (Robson and Wright, 1989; Visser, 1991).

DEVELOPMENT OF A MODULAR COURSE

The need for rigorous management of such a process of training has created the possibility for increased partnerships between LEAs and institutions. The partnership in Humberside has reached a high degree of sophistication with the LEA working very closely with Hull University. These developments have been closely monitored by Her Majesty's Inspectors (HMI) and external examiners and have been informed by several formative course evaluations (Hornby, 1990), in addition to two surveys of the competencies required for working with pupils with SEN (Holland and Hornby, 1992; Hornby *et al.*, 1991).

Currently almost 200 Humberside teachers are registered on award-bearing courses in special educational needs. The overwhelming majority of these are enrolled on the SEN Modular Advanced Diploma course offered in partnership by Humberside LEA and Hull University. A seventh cohort of 50 students started the course in September 1993. As with earlier cohorts, these students are drawn from mainstream primary and secondary schools, colleges of further education, special schools, learning support services and units in mainstream schools. The majority of those enrolled in recent years work in mainstream schools or in the LEA's Learning Support Service, with a small number from special schools.

This diversity in the teaching backgrounds of the students is mirrored by those staff who deliver the course modules. These include educational psychologists, Health Authority staff, LEA advisers, teachers, further education lecturers, special school headteachers, heads of LEA support services and university staff. More than 40 tutors teach on the 25 modules currently available on the course. This cocktail of talents ensures that students benefit from the expertise of a wide range of practitioners, as well as receiving an infusion of academic rigour. Coordination is provided by a member of the advisory service with a specific brief for the programme, and a management committee. The management committee consists of LEA and University staff and representatives from course tutors and students.

Modes of delivery are similarly diverse and require considerable commitment from students themselves in terms of their own time. The previous system of one-year secondments to gain a diploma in SEN has disappeared from Humberside, except for mandatory training for teachers of the hearing impaired, and has been replaced by a range of short-term secondments to Hull University, contact-time sessions, 'twilight' hours training, residential weekends, and distance learning. In the past the LEA could support only 15 teachers on full-time secondments for SEN award-bearing courses, whereas this new mode of delivery allows a much larger number of teachers the opportunity to achieve an award, albeit with a greater investment of time from themselves. The course, however, being modular, offers students a greater choice in that they can take up to five years to complete it.

The commitment of students and tutors is matched by the County Council's financial support for the course. Although the LEA receives a proportion of the costs from the Department for Education, these moneys would not be sufficient to support a course as ambitious as this. County councillors have voted substantial funds to ensure that this initiative is protected from the vagaries and uncertainties of central funding. This, of course, does not protect the course from the recommendations of the Boundary Commission concerning Humberside or the implications of the council tax and the possibility of charge-capping.

COURSE STRUCTURE

The Advanced Diploma in SEN consists of nine, 30-hour, taught modules (each with an assignment or assignments), a child-focused project file and an institution-focused study. To ensure that students are allowed an element of choice yet still cover fundamental areas of special education, there is a mixture of compulsory and optional modules at the different levels of the course. The four levels, leading to different degrees of award, are described below and in Figure 4.1.

First is the *foundation level*, which leads to an LEA Certificate in Special Educational Needs and is compulsory for all students. This part of the course consists of three modules designated A, B, and C, delivered over an academic year, and is the basic level of training the LEA recommends for a SEN coordinator in a mainstream school or college. The LEA aims to ensure that one teacher from every primary and three from every secondary school undertake this level of training. For the past seven years, 50 to 60 teachers per year have started the foundation level.

The content, designed to replicate and replace the earlier Department of Education and Science (DES) 20-day courses and complementing the LEA's published SEN policy, reflects this aim.

- Module A, a residential weekend, introduces students to each other and to the LEA's three-stage assessment procedures under the 1981 Act. Participants are given an opportunity to work through real examples of referrals and documentation brought before the LEA statementing panel.
- Module B informs students about the type and range of resources available to support pupils within other institutions such as special schools or support services.
- Module C deals in more detail with the techniques of identification, assessment and intervention.

Both of modules B and C, with the exception of the visits, are delivered out of directed time, that is outside working hours. They are, however, offered simultaneously in different parts of Humberside to ensure equal access for teachers across the county.

Finally, students combine and synthesize their experiences from the three foundation modules by completing a project file based on a child or group of children known to them.

Approximately two-thirds of students move on to the second level which leads to the *University of Hull's Certificate in Special Educational Needs*. Two more modules, described as professional modules, are chosen from a menu of 15.

These modules include sensory disabilities, severe learning difficulties, life skills programmes, information technology, language difficulties, and post-16 issues.

Figure 4.1: *Structure of modular course*

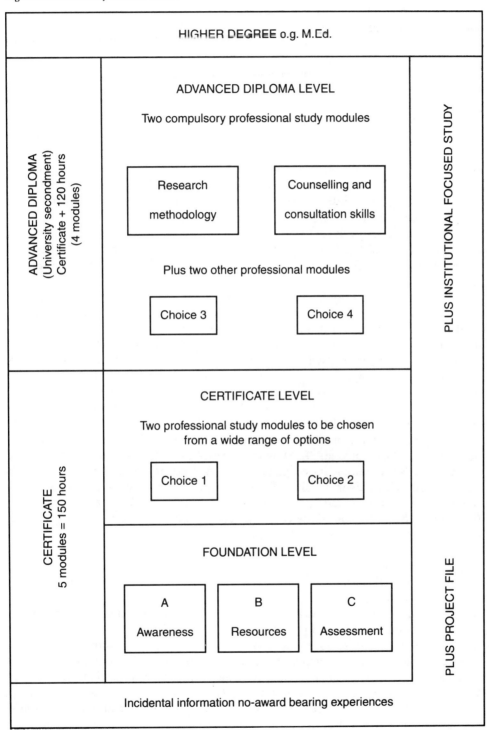

Although some of these modules are delivered in part during school hours, they are normally offered outside directed time. They are also open to teachers on a 'buy-in' basis; that is, places not taken up by modular course students are filled by other teachers. Over 100 teachers a year are able to participate in the modules on such a basis. In this way the modular course also provides the LEA with a convenient vehicle for a wide-ranging programme of SEN training.

The third level, the *University Advanced Diploma in SEN*, is taken during an eight-week secondment to the university.

Between 15 and 20 students a year follow the course through to this level. Proportionally, teachers in special schools or units and learning support service members make up the majority of those who progress this far. At diploma level all students take two compulsory modules which are delivered by university staff: a module on counselling and consultation skills for working with parents and other professionals, and another on research methodology. The latter helps prepare students for their institution-focused study which they will complete in the months following the secondment. In addition, they take two other optional modules from a menu of four including complex learning difficulties and emotional and behavioural difficulties. There are further opportunities for visiting other educational establishments during the secondment.

The aim of the institution-focused study is to enable course members to implement some of what they have learned on the course in their own schools or colleges. Through conducting these studies it is intended that course members should be influential in bringing about constructive changes in provision for SEN in their own institutions.

Examples of topics chosen for institutional-focused studies are: whole-school approaches to spelling, disability awareness, truancy, parent involvement, whole-school approaches to bullying and evaluating integration programmes.

Following completion of the Advanced Diploma, a small number of students each year move on to the *Hull University's Master of Education (MEd) programme in SEN* – the fourth level in the modular course structure. Five or six students per year have done so for the last four years. The university can allow exemption from up to one half of the master's programme in recognition of work done on the Advanced Diploma in SEN course. The university also allows exemption from up to four modules of certificate level for prior training in SEN at an approved institution of higher education. In addition, the validation of the course by Hull University facilitates credit transfer should teachers move to another LEA before completing the course.

DIFFERENT ROUTES

At Advanced Diploma level students may opt for one of three routes to the final award: generic; emotional and behavioural difficulties; or complex (severe) learning difficulties. Teachers who choose not to specialize in their choice of professional modules will receive a generic qualification in SEN. However, if they should choose all four of their optional modules in the area of emotional and behavioural difficulties, or complex learning difficulties, their final award will acknowledge either of these specialisms. Most students opt for the generic route although the emotional and behavioural difficulty modules are extremely popular and a significant number choose that route.

The complex learning difficulties route is in its second year and, along with most institutions of higher education that offer courses in severe learning difficulties, the university is at present experiencing problems in recruiting on to the course.

FEEDBACK

Although the course is managed by LEA and university administrators, it is overseen and monitored by a management committee composed of LEA and university delegates together with tutor and student representatives. Each module of the course is evaluated using a standard questionnaire and regular reports, based on the evaluations, are submitted to the management committee. In the first and third year of the university secondment, students taking part were interviewed in depth, all of this supplementing annual visits of the external examiner who has met with students and tutors on each of those occasions. This feedback has been used to modify the structure and content of the course considerably.

Feedback from students suggests that, for most participants, the motivation for taking the course is a blend of professional development and career aspiration. Most are keen to gain a recognized qualification as it is seen as a way of establishing professional credibility with peers and, because of the high status with which the LEA regards the award, as a means of career advancement. Most hope the course will increase their knowledge of classroom practice as well as giving them a wider perspective on special education. Interviews with students in the final stages of their studies suggest that these objectives are considered to be well met by the course (Hornby, 1990).

Many also consider that the modular structure is an advantage when it comes to the choice and flexibility it allows for personal circumstances. However, the emphasis on 'twilight sessions' at foundation and certificate level is generally seen as a disadvantage. Following a taxing day in the classroom, it is hard to concentrate. Students report this particularly regarding didactic presentations. They generally prefer tutors who allow opportunities for discussion and practical activities. Even at the end of a working day, teachers prefer active rather than inactive learning. The short-term secondment to Hull University is appreciated by all who progress to that level and some have commented on the fact that being a practitioner while taking the course, rather than out of the classroom for a year, allows more direct linking of assignments to classroom practice.

Because of the large number of students involved, the variety and size of the tutoring team, the 3512 square miles comprising Humberside, and the fact that two large institutions need to cooperate to an unprecedented degree, there have been some teething problems. Early cohorts were particularly critical of the administrative side of the course: many felt that communication was poor, especially with regard to the advertising of modules. Feedback from later cohorts suggests that communication has been improved by the appointment of both a part-time course secretary and a member of the advisory service with a specific brief for the course, as well as by the introduction of a regular course newsletter. The LEA and the university have also had time to mesh their disparate systems more closely and to understand each other's mentalities.

Another regular complaint has been that assignments sometimes take a long time to be returned to students after submission. This is due to the fact that most of the tutors, being full-time practitioners themselves, have other commitments. Perhaps this is an unavoidable consequence of receiving tuition from those with classroom credibility. This is another area which is currently being considered by the management committee.

Where next? The structure is continuing to develop in terms of the number of modules offered; for example the area of reading difficulties is currently being considered as a new module. The programme is now open to careers officers as full participants. Good communication with other institutions of higher education in neighbouring LEAs and compatibility of course structures have always been aspects of the course. It is intended that even closer relationships can be developed. Distance learning has been trialled in the past as an alternative strategy for delivering one module, and it is being considered again as a possible way forward for the course to reach more students locally, regionally and nationally. In particular, it is being considered whether the modules in complex learning difficulties and dyslexia could be marketed by this means.

The main features of the course are the unique relationship between the LEA and the university, and the acceptance that training is most effective if delivered by credible, active professionals and is clearly related to day-to-day in-school activity (Johnson and Wright, 1992). Both of these factors have provided challenges for the organization and management of the modular course. Attempting to meet these challenges has led to the development of a course structure and management strategies which have greatly improved in-service training in SEN in Humberside.

REFERENCES

Dean. J. (1989) *Special Needs in the Secondary School: The Whole School Approach*. London: Routledge.
DES (1978) *Education of Handicapped Children and Young People (Warnock Report)*. London: HMSO.
Hodgson, F. and Trotter, A. (1989) 'In-service education and special needs'. In N. Jones and T. Southgate (eds) *The Management of Special Needs in Ordinary Schools*. London: Routledge.
Holland, J. and Hornby, G. (1992) 'Competencies for teachers of children with special educational needs: a comparison of teachers' ratings with those of senior professionals'. *British Journal of In-service Education*, **18**(1), 59–62.
Hornby, G. (1990) 'A modular approach to training'. *British Journal of Special Education*, **17**(4), 156–60.
Hornby, G. (1992) 'Integration of children with special educational needs: is it time for a policy review?' *Support for Learning*, **7**(3), 130–4.
Hornby, G., Wickham, P. and Zielinski, A. (1991) 'Establishing competencies for training teachers of children with special educational needs'. *European Journal of Special Needs Education*, **6**(1), 30–36.
Johnson, M. and Wright, M. (1992) 'A unique partnership'. *Special Children*, **57**, 34–6.
Roaf, C. (1991) 'Whole school policies: a question of rights?' In N. Jones and T. Southgate (eds) *The Management of Special Needs in Ordinary Schools*, London: Routledge.
Robson, C. and Wright, M. (1989) 'SEN: towards a modular pattern of INSET'. *Support for Learning*, **4**(2), 83–9.

Smith, C.J. (1992) 'Management of special needs'. In T. Gulliford and G. Upton (eds) *Special Educational Needs*. London: Routledge.

Visser, J. (1991) 'In-service courses: staff development and special educational needs'. In M. Hinson (ed.) *Teachers and Special Educational Needs*. Harlow: Longman.

Wright, M. (1989) 'INSET; the role of the special school'. In D. Baker and K. Bovair (eds) *Making the Special Schools Ordinary*, Volume 1. London: Falmer Press.

Chapter 5

The In-service Training Needs of Primary Teachers for Integration in Spain

M. Jesus Balbás

This chapter provides a synthesis of research which has been carried out in the University of Seville in Spain. It deals with the training needs of the regular integration teachers, in other words, primary school teachers who have children with special needs in their classes (Balbás, 1993).

First of all the research team carried out a broad theoretical review of this subject starting from a firm theoretical and experimental base. In this chapter I aim to summarize our research process, including the collection and analysis of data, the most important results and our final conclusions.

BASIC ASSUMPTIONS AND RESEARCH AIMS

Our investigation started from several basic assumptions, of which three are of special importance. The first is that integration in the primary school must be perceived as an innovation which involves a change of school structures and raises serious questions which have to be answered (Hegarty, 1987; Zabalza and Parrilla, 1991; López Melero, 1990, 1991; Parrilla 1992a, 1992b). There are new conditions appearing in schools which regular, special and support teachers have to take into account. Since the middle of the 1970s the relationship between regular and special education has been improving. As a result, new situations have arisen which urgently need to be investigated (Leyser and Abrams, 1986; Birch and Reynolds, 1982). One of the needs which school integration involves is the training of teachers who are already in the education system, that is, the continuous training of teaching staff who have previous experience (Crisci, 1981; Powers, 1983; Mittler, 1986; Upton, 1991).

Secondly, there are important training needs among all teacher groups in primary and secondary schools when pupils with special needs join their classes. Usually the teachers, above all regular teachers, do not consider themselves ready to undertake integration in their classrooms, nor do they have either the knowledge or the skills which would enable them to face up to integration and to offer suitable attention to children with special needs (Crisci, 1981; Leyser and Abrams 1986; Reynolds, 1990;

Stainback and Stainback, 1984; Jones, 1989). It is obvious that there is an important in-service training need for every teacher (Grant and Secada, 1990). This training must be carried out urgently, because, according to Reynolds and Birch (1977), the professional development of experienced teachers is progressing much more slowly than the efforts that are being made to situate children with special needs in regular classes.

We must give priority to in-service training of regular teachers in order that they should accept the responsibility to teach children with special needs. An aspect of in-service training which can help to give it relevance and meaning is that it starts from the needs of the teachers. Programmes of professional development usually have great success when the results obtained match well with the teachers' perceived needs (Iwanicki and McEachern, 1984; Robson *et al.*, 1988). Our third basic assumption is therefore that regular teachers are able to think about the situation in which they are working, evaluate it and so identify their own training needs (Montero, 1987; Iwanicki and McEachern, 1984).

In this context, our research had these aims:

1. to identify the training needs of primary school teachers if they are to receive these children in their classrooms;
2. to identify the features which have to be included in the in-service training of teachers involved in integration;
3. to identify the general lines for an in-service training programme which would respond to these needs.

We tried to achieve a mainly descriptive identification, with the aim of responding practically to an actual situation in a particular region.

We also set ourselves a methodological objective, with the intention of confirming that the combination of data gathering and analysis in both quantitative and qualitative ways can be of great advantage and convenience for our approach to day-to-day reality. We tried in fact to overcome the dichotomy between qualitative and quantitative methods (Stromquist, 1983; Cook and Reichardt, 1986; Lincoln, 1988; Hegarty and Evans, 1988).

THE RESEARCH PROCESS

The global process of our research was this. We first undertook a theoretical review that enabled us to establish our research aims and hypotheses. Having chosen our data collection strategies, we were able to design and administer both interviews and questionnaires. Qualitative analysis of interview data and quantitative analysis of the data from the questionnaires produced the results and general conclusions on which we have been able to base a proposal for an in-service training programme.

THE SAMPLE

We divided those who took part in the sample into two groups: those to be interviewed and those to whom we sent questionnaires. The former (the interview group) consisted of 17 key informants, chosen by virtue of their experience in integration and their professional role (regular teachers, support teachers, principals and officials of local authorities). The latter (the questionnaire group) included all the primary school teachers in the Seville area who had children with special needs integrated in their classes. They had to be teaching in state schools operating official integration projects. We received 360 questionnaires from this group.

DATA COLLECTION

We ourselves devised both the interviews and the questionnaires. The questionnaires were based on the theoretical review and on information collected from the interviews. The interviews conducted with the 17 chosen informants were guided and open-ended.

The questionnaire enabled us to approach a large number of people. Entitled 'Teacher training needs arising from integration' it consisted of three independent sections: Identification Data, General Knowledge and Organizational Preferences. The answer form was of the Likert-scale kind, with four options.

The first section (Identification Data) was intended to elicit demographic information about the teachers and the schools.

In the second section (General Knowledge) we tried to assess the training needs arising from different educational contexts. We decided to do this in an indirect way by examining the discrepancy between the importance teachers attached to a particular training need and the amount of training available to them. The questionnaire therefore distinguished between two answer scales for each item: importance and training level.

The content of General Knowledge was divided into five major theoretical dimensions:

- general knowledge about integration and special education;
- adaptation of teaching;
- evaluation and assessment;
- relationships and cooperation within the teaching community;
- self-assessment and professional development.

The third section concerned Organizational Preferences for in-service courses: when and where to hold them, who should take charge of them, characteristics, obstacles, and so on.

DATA ANALYSIS

We need to distinguish between the techniques used for the qualitative analysis of interviews and the quantitative measures used for the questionnaires.

For the interviews we used the technique established by Miles and Huberman (1984) through matrix and content analysis. We worked with different sorts of matrix, depending on the distinct patterns of analysis that we intended to achieve. This was done on three levels: descriptive, interpretative and comparative.

The information obtained from the questionnaires was submitted to several kinds of statistical analysis. We may distinguish two large experimental groups: for validity and reliability, the Cronbach Alpha and factorial analysis; for the analysis of descriptive data and hypothesis contrast, frequencies and rate analysis, the differential test between pairs of Wilcoxon, analysis of variance and 'Student's *t*'.

RESULTS

The interviews

Presenting these results means that we have to make use of broad thematic categories which were designed to achieve the first descriptive analysis: perceptions; implications; limitations; conditions; training needs; characteristics.

First of all, referring to *perceptions*, what sense do the respondents give to the word 'integration' or how do they interpret it? The answer can be reduced to one sentence: 'Integration is living like others.'

With regard to the *implications* of integration, there were three main groups. One concerned necessary adaptations – of the individual, of the organization, of relationships. The second covered coordination, the need for a supporting teacher and the role of specialists and other partners. The third concerned feelings, for example fear, distress, insecurity, educational discomfort.

Among the perceived *limitations* of the integrational process, the most representative were the level of training, the willingness of teaching staff and their isolation, and restraints imposed by the administration.

As for the *conditions* which the respondents considered necessary for the implementation of integration, the emphasis was on coordination, training, attitudes and support.

Training needs were not easily identified. The following were mentioned: knowledge about the characteristics of disabilities; a global vision of the pupil's possible handicaps; planning to meet individual needs; general knowledge about integration.

Finally, there were certain *characteristics* which in-service training should have in order to meet the needs of teachers. It should take place during the school timetable and at or near the teacher's own school. It should be given by experts on several topics from inside and outside the school itself, and should respond to expressed needs. It should be provided over an extended period and should have continuity. Teachers themselves should contribute to its design and development.

In general, teachers expressed more negative than positive views about their in-service training.

The questionnaire

The reliability of the test results was 0.949 for the Importance scale and 0.963 for the Training scale. These results suggest that the questionnaire presents a high level of internal reliability and consistency.

I shall give a brief synthesis of the results of the *descriptive analysis*, but first I must emphasize that the responses stressed the vital importance of teacher training for the successful realization of integration.

The regular teachers considered all the statements in the questionnaire to be very important for the integration process. They mainly emphasized the adaptation of teaching, relationships and cooperation within the teaching community, and assessment and evaluation. Elements judged less important included general knowledge of integration and special education, and self-assessment and professional development.

When it comes to the level of training available, teachers think of themselves as having very limited training or no training at all on most of the topics covered by the questionnaire. Within this general tendency, the areas in which they consider themselves to be better trained are self-assessment and professional development, and assessment and evaluation. They consider themselves to be at a lower level of training in general knowledge about integration and special education and in adaptation of teaching.

As for the organizational aspects, the most important obstacle stressed was the lack of time to achieve the training objectives, followed by long distances and unsuitable timetables. Teachers prefer to carry out training during school hours and at their own place of work; it should be funded by the school administration. Trainers should be specialists in the various areas of special education; next in importance are multiprofessional groups and the teachers' own colleagues. The training should be organized by the Teachers' Centre, in coordination with the primary schools.

Training should focus on improvements in classroom practice and in the development of educational materials and resources. Finally, these in-service training activities for integration should be extended to the classroom. They have to be designed with teachers, and to be practical and close to reality.

At the beginning of the research we developed four major hypotheses that would be investigated by means of the questionnaire. These are the results.

Hypothesis 1 was intended to investigate training needs, relying on the discrepancy between training priorities and availability. For that purpose, we used the Wilcoxon ranked pairs test. The differences between all the compared pairs turned out to be highly significant. By this means we checked out the existence of important training needs among the regular teachers in primary schools in the Seville area having children with special educational needs in their classes.

Hypotheses 2, 3 and 4 led us to the study of the influence on the self-assessment that the teachers apply to their training of certain (respectively) personal, academic and professional characteristics: age, teaching experience, level at which they are teaching, experience in integration and in-service training activities, and achievement in relation to integration.

Through the analysis of variables (ANOVA) and the 'Student's *t*' test we could establish that very few variables have a significant influence on the teachers' self-perceptions.

Three of the chosen variables – age, teaching experience and the level at which the respondents were teaching – were not related to the five dimensions. Experience in integration was significant in three out of five dimensions: general knowledge about

integration and special education, teaching adaptation, and relationships and cooperation within the teaching community.

GENERAL CONCLUSIONS

The research emphasizes the importance of designing training programmes which are
relevant to the perceived needs of teachers. There are five specific conclusions:

1. Our most important conclusion is that it is necessary to revise the teacher training
   programmes which have been developed so far in order to prepare professionals to
   respond to diversity in the classroom. It is also necessary to revise the training
   programmes based on categories: training programmes have to be more responsive to individual needs.
2. In-service teacher training needs to be considered as part of the teacher's job,
   rather than as an optional activity.
3. There is no agreement within the teaching community on the skills and com-
   petences which are essential to successful integrated teaching, whether this
   teaching is provided by mainstream teachers, support teachers or specialists.
4. The need for separate initial training for general and specialist teachers was
   questioned.
5. There are clear coincidences between the topics that we identified in our initial
   theoretical review of the needs of teachers facing integration and the ones we have
   discovered in our research. These topics relate to the curriculum and its adaptation, the detection of pupils with special educational needs, and the relationships
   and cooperation among the members of the teaching community (Balbás, 1994).

REFERENCES

Balbás. M.J. (1993) Las necesidades formativas del profesor tutor de E.G.B. ante la integración:
   Evaluación diagnóstica y propuesta de formación. Unpublished PhD thesis, University of
   Seville.
Balbás, M.J. (1994) *La Formación Permanente del Profesorado ante La Integración*. Barcelona:
   P.P.U.
Birch. J.W. and Reynolds. M.C. (1982) 'Special education as a profession'. *Exceptional
   Education Quarterly,* **2**(4), 1–13.
Cook. T.D. and Reichardt. C.S. (1986) *Métodos Cualitativos y Cuantitativos en Investigación
   Evaluativa,* Madrid: Morata.
Crisci, P.T. (1981) 'Competencies for mainstreaming: problems and issues'. *Education and
   Training of the Mentally Retarded,* **16**(3). 175–82.
Grant. C. and Secada. G. (1990) 'Preparing teachers for diversity'. In R. Houston (ed.)
   Handbook of Research in Teacher Education. New York: Macmillan.
Hegarty, S. (1987) *Meeting Special Needs in Ordinary Schools.* London: Cassell.
Hegarty, S. and Evans. P. (1988) *Research and Evaluation Methods in Special Education.*
   Windsor: NFER-Nelson.
Iwanicki, E.F. and McEachern, L. (1984) 'Using teacher self-assessment to identify staff develop-
   ment needs'. *Journal of Teacher Education,* **35**(2), 38–45.
Jones, S.D. (1989) 'Content of special education courses for pre-service regular education
   teachers'. *Teacher Education and Special Education,* **12**(4), 154–9.
Leyser, Y. and Abrams, T. (1986) 'Perceived training needs of regular and special education
   student teachers in the area of mainstreaming'. *The Exceptional Child,* **33**(3), 173–80.

Lincoln, Y.S. (1988) 'The role of ideology in naturalistic research'. Paper presented at symposium: Ideology in Qualitative Research Methodologies. New Orleans.

López Melero, M. (1990) *La Integración Escolar: Otra Cultura*. Málaga: Cuadernos de Puertanueva.

López Melero, M. (1991) 'La formación necesaria en una escuela de la diversidad: propuesta de cara a los nuevos planes de estudio'. In M.A. Zabalza and J.R. Alberte (eds) *Educación Especial y Formación de Profesores*. Santiago: Turculo.

Miles, M.B. and Huberman, A.M. (1984) *Qualitative Data Analysis*. London: Sage Publications.

Mittler, P. (1986) 'The new look in in-service training'. *British Journal of Special Education*, **13** 50–1.

Montero, L. (1987) 'Las necesidades formativas de los profesores como enfoque de la formación en servicio: análisis de una investigación'. *Revista de Investigación Educativa*, **5**(9), 7–31.

Parrilla, A. (1992a) *La Integración Escolar como Experiencia Institucional*. Seville: G.I.D.

Parrilla, A. (1992b) *La Integración Escolar y los Profesores: Investigación y Formación*. Madrid: Cincel-Kapelusz.

Powers, D.A. (1983) 'Mainstreaming and the inservice education of teachers'. *Exceptional Children*, **49**(5), 432–9.

Reynolds, M. (1990) 'Educating teachers for special education students.' In W. Robert Houston (ed.) *Handbook of Research on Teacher Education*. New York: Macmillan, 423–36.

Reynolds. M. and Birch. J. (1977) *Teaching Exceptional Children in all America's Schools*. Reston: Council for Exceptional Children.

Robson. C., Sebba, J. and Mittler. P. (1988) *In-service Training and Special Needs: Running Short School-Focused Courses*. Manchester: Manchester University Press.

Stainback. W. and Stainback. S. (1984) 'Preparing regular class teachers for the integration of severely retarded students'. *Education and Training of the Mentally Retarded*, **17**(4), 273–7.

Stromquist. N. (1983) 'La relación entre los enfoques cualitativos y cuantitativos'. International seminar on the process of interpretation in qualitative research of the educational scene. Bogata.

Upton. G (ed.) (1991) *Staff Training and Special Educational Needs*. London: David Fulton.

Zabalza. M.A. and Parrilla. A. (1991) 'La organización escolar frente a la integración'. In J. López and B. Bermejo (eds) *El Centro Educativo*. Seville: G.I.D.

Chapter 6

Special Education in Italy: Integration of People with Disabilities and the Education of the Teachers

Renzo Vianello and Silvia Moniga

INTRODUCTION

In order to understand the education of teachers for special needs in Italy, we need first to consider the education of the children themselves.

For this reason the first three parts of this chapter will concern the school integration of children with disabilities (or *severe* learning difficulties), the situation of children defined as having learning difficulties, and a teaching proposal for a class where children with and without (more or less severe) learning difficulties are included.

Most of the chapter will concern the education of ordinary and support teachers, and the final part will be dedicated to proposals regarding teachers' in-service training.

The education of children with special needs in Italy has a number of characteristics. Nearly all the children with mental disability are integrated in ordinary classes: there is moreover a clear distinction between the situation of children with severe or rather severe disability and that of children with less severe learning difficulties; and although there is a high percentage of support teachers, ordinary teachers are directly involved in special education. In drawing the attention of non-Italian readers to these aspects we are inviting them to consider particular characteristics of the Italian situation as part of a complex system.

THE SCHOOL INTEGRATION OF DISABLED CHILDREN

The population of Italy is just over 57.5 million (1993 figures). Children up to the age of 18 number about 11 million, children aged from 6 to 14 (the years in which it is compulsory to attend school) about 5.6 million. There are about 100,000 disabled children aged 6 to 14. About thirty years ago a high percentage of these children were taught in special schools or special classes; the aim was to offer special opportunities to 20 per cent of the pupils. Now almost all pupils are integrated in normal classes. In the school year 1993–94, 98.5 per cent of the children with disabilities were integrated, that is about 1 or 2 disabled pupils for every 100 peers.

In Italy only a very small percentage of pupils is considered disabled, 1.8 per cent of the population of schoolchildren. In some countries, for example England, Denmark and Norway, it is more common to use the expression 'children with special needs', or 'pupils with learning difficulties' rather than 'pupils with disability (or handicap)', without distinguishing the pupils with severe difficulties from the others. Of course the use of different labels makes it difficult to compare the situations in various countries.

In some respects this may be only a formal problem. For example, children with learning difficulties exist in Italy too, but they are not labelled as disabled pupils. In other respects the difference is important, since from these labels derive teaching policies. In Italy, for example, not all pupils traditionally defined as 'mildly mentally retarded' but only the more severe among these (those with an IQ lower than 60–65) are taught by a support teacher. This means that many pupils who in other countries would normally be considered 'disabled' or 'with (very) severe special needs' in Italy are not only integrated in regular classes but are also taught by ordinary teachers.

In order to make a comparison, we can mention some percentages of pupils who are considered disabled (or with special needs or with learning difficulties) and who, for at least a part of their time in school, have the help of support teachers (in other words, in special education) in various countries (Vianello, 1992): 1.8 per cent in Italy (Vianello, 1989b): 4 per cent in Belgium (Lamoral, 1991); 5–6 per cent in France, Norway and Switzerland (Bernath and Kayser, 1991; Filippini Steinemann, 1991; Gugelmann, 1989; Helimäki, 1991; Østli, 1990, 1991); 7 per cent in the Netherlands (Breur and Breur de Ru, 1989; EASE, 1991); 9 per cent in the USA (Danielson and Bellamy, 1988; US Department of Education, 1988; Vitello, 1989); 10 per cent in Sweden (Rosenqvist, in press); 13 per cent in Denmark (Jacobsen, 1989); 20 per cent in Portugal (Da Fonseca, 1991), and in England and Wales (Mittler and Farrell, 1987; Mittler, 1988).

Another interesting comparison is possible if we look at the percentages of pupils attending special schools or special classes: less than 0.1 per cent in Italy, less than 1 per cent in Sweden, 1–2 per cent in Norway, about 2 per cent in Denmark and in England and Wales, 3–4 per cent in some *Länder* of Germany (Preuss, 1990; Wenz, 1991), in Belgium (Lamoral, 1991), in Greece (Stasinos, 1991) and in the USA and 7 per cent in the Netherlands (Netherlands Ministry of Education and Science, 1989).

As regards Italy the breakdown by categories of impairment is shown in Table 6.1 overleaf (Vianello, 1994; Vianello and Moniga, 1994).

Support teachers, that is teachers who look after disabled pupils in ordinary schools, number just over 42,000 in compulsory education (school year 1993–94). On average the ratio is one support teacher to 2.2 disabled pupils.

In Italy the maximum number of children per class is 25. In other words with 26 pupils, two classes of 13 are established. If a disabled pupil is integrated, and it is not permitted to integrate more than one per class, the maximum number of the other pupils becomes 19.

Nearly a quarter of the classes (22.5 per cent) have a disabled pupil integrated, and so have no more than 20 pupils. In such cases, therefore, these pupils benefit from a full-time teacher (or even more), and of another teacher for a further average of nine hours, depending on the severity of the disability. Between the years 1980–81 and 1989–90 the decrease in the number of pupils per teacher in the pre-school was from 13.1 to 10.8;

Table 6.1 *Categories of impairment among disabled children in Italy*

Disabled pupils	Percentage of normal peers	Percentage of disabled peers
Visually impaired	0.04	2
Hearing impaired	0.11	6
Physically disabled	0.25	14
Mentally retarded	1.00	56
Emotionally disturbed	0.25	14
Multiple/various	0.15	8
Total	1.80	100

from 1980–81 to 1990–91, the decrease was from 15.7 to 10.5 in the elementary school, from 10.5 to 8.2 in the junior school and from 10.1 to 9.4 in the senior high school.

Support teachers can work with full-time teachers with the whole class, but they may also teach in a resource room with the disabled pupil, alone or with other non-disabled pupils. The practice of forming a group composed of two or more disabled pupils is rare.

To understand the Italian situation it is useful to consider another aspect. Generally both teachers and parents, including parents of children without a disability, favour integration. Integration in Italy was made possible by the lack of resistance, or at least by minimal resistance, on the part of parents of normal children.

This has been shown in objective surveys too. Vianello (1988, 1989a, 1990b) carried out several investigations in this field. One of these, concluded only recently, compared the results of a questionnaire (Larrivee and Cook, 1979) completed by regular teachers and head teachers in the USA, Australia and Italy. The attitude of Italian teachers, both regular and specialized, and of headteachers, towards the integration of disabled pupils, proved to be more positive than that of their foreign colleagues.

In our opinion, experience and research about school integration in Italy suggest that integration in normal classes is productive only if certain conditions are met. These are:

- only one disabled pupil per class (in other countries the average is two or more);
- no more than 20 pupils in total per class:
- the help of a support teacher for at least 6–8 hours per week;
- the collaboration of all the staff of the school.

The following have proved very useful, if not essential:

- adequate collaboration with those working in the health service, such as psychologists, neuropsychiatrists and social workers;
- the presence of an educational psychologist in the school;
- the favourable attitude, or at least not a hostile attitude, of parents of the other pupils:
- the practice of comparing notes systematically among teachers;
- the involvement of regular teachers in planning and applying the Learning Programme for the disabled pupil;
- a knowledge among teachers of the normal development of the various aspects of personality, in order that they may also realize what is normal in exceptional situations;

- the capacity to formulate polyfunctional didactic proposals, for example how one should proceed in a class with pupils of different ages:
- the practice, during normal didactic activity, of working in small groups.

Pupils with learning difficulties

So it is clear that in Italy many opportunities are provided to favour school integration of children with more or less severe disabilities. Less clear is the situation of children who have learning difficulties without being mentally handicapped – children with impairment in the development of learning skills (reading, writing, arithmetic) not accounted for by chronological age, mental age or inadequate schooling. Language disorders or impairment in motor coordination may also be included. These impairments may also be caused or accompanied by attention disorders together with hyperactivity.

In these cases a support teacher is not provided, and the learning difficulties of these children tend to be underestimated by teachers. General remarks about learning disorders can be found in school legislation but without any actual provisions.

In general, research carried out by the University of Padua (for example Cornoldi, 1991; Vianello, 1994) has shown that in Italy children with learning disorders are more numerous than those considered disabled: while, as we have seen, about 1.8 per cent of the school population is reckoned as having a disability, 2.4 per cent are considered to have learning difficulties.

Learning disorders in Italy are considered to come within the province of normality, even if on the borderline of this. To enable a comparison with the situation of children with disabilities, it would seem helpful to describe briefly what generally happens when one or more children with learning difficulties are present in a class. We can consider two contexts of intervention: within the school and outside it.

Inside the school, the psychopedagogue is one of the professional figures expected to be involved with learning disorders. Psychopedagogues have a university degree in learning processes and disorders and, among other things, should be responsible for the planning and coordination of educational intervention in case of difficulties. However, legislation regarding these professionals is very confused and their presence inside the school is rare.

In practice most of the children with learning disorders are referred to the local health and social departments (USSL) for a diagnosis of the specific type of learning disorder. Inside these departments the presence of a psychopedagogue is rare, and generally the diagnosis is carried out by a psychologist and/or a neuropsychiatrist who is also responsible for any rehabilitation. In some cases the intervention is implemented in collaboration with the school. Rarely a different educational project within the class is specified or regular meetings of teachers with the staff of the Health and Social Department are arranged.

Didactic proposals for a class in which pupils with special needs are integrated

Teaching children with special needs integrated in a normal class requires specific didactics. A support teacher, if one is available, can work together with the curricular teacher in the same room or in another room. He or she can teach the pupil with special needs alone or together with other children. In both cases, for some hours (often more than half of the school time) the pupil with special needs has to be taught together with all the other pupils in the class. This involves problems that are difficult to solve on both an organizational and a didactic level. A teacher of mathematics, for example, although doing everything with great care, may meet with various failures through using the same specific topics for the whole class. By planning a series of gradual steps in logical progression they might hope slowly to guide the pupil with severe learning difficulties to an understanding of the physical laws or processes of mathematical reasoning. But this approach will have disadvantages. First, this process may turn out to be too long, and too boring, for the majority of the pupils; secondly, the pupil with learning difficulties is placed in a situation of passive learning, being obliged merely to follow a predetermined path.

Our didactic proposals have been elaborated precisely to overcome, at least in part, these difficulties. We must stress that our model can be considered particularly appropriate when children with more or less severe learning difficulties are integrated in a regular school class.

The first characteristic of our proposal is the use of general topics, chosen in order to permit the pupils to perform at various levels of complexity. For example, the topics can be attacked merely at the oral level, or also by means of drawing, or using the written word too. The topic has to be 'rich', presented in a way that permits the teacher to offer many stimuli that reflect upon it. The topic presented should be treated for at least 10 to 15 hours. It is useful to divide the work into three phases: the collection of experiences and materials, individual or small group work, and finally a general synthesis, possibly with the production of a concrete result such as a booklet or some wall posters.

Our experience suggests topics such as a season, my city or country, a job, a means of transport, the sea, the mountains, animals. A suitable choice of between five and ten topics can allow the main programming of the work during the hours in which both the support and the curricular teacher are present. In order to work in this way teachers have to elaborate a working programme coherent with both the special needs of the particular pupil and the general work of the other pupils.

It is effective to alternate individual work and group work; normally the group work is useful in order to collect ideas, experiences, materials and techniques, while the individual work is useful for production. Between work with the whole class and individual work there is work in small groups, a modality which we consider most important. In a class where a pupil with special needs is integrated, four or five groups of five children each would be appropriate. Aspects to be considered for effective work in small groups are as follows:

- Groups should be formed on criteria aimed at favouring individual social development.
- An outline of the work should be provided for each group, coherent with the one provided for the other groups and complementary to it, elaborated by the teachers but prepared and discussed with the group.
- A request for a 'material' conclusion of the work should be made.
- A final reporter for each group should be chosen.

- Respect for the principle of speaking one after the other in discussions should first be established and then ensured.
- The activity of the groups is to be controlled so as to favour the involvement of all the members.
- A large amount of time should be devoted to the third phase, which is the presentation of the work to the other groups.

To help the group to work efficiently, the teacher will have to offer, and let the children discover, instruments for the collection of information and for 'materializing' the results, but without taking the place of the pupils as regards content. The role of the teacher as 'transmitter of contents' is postponed to the conclusion of the group work, as a response to any problems that have arisen.

We consider work in groups as especially important for the aims of integration, for two main reasons. First, it can begin when the specialized and curricular teachers are working simultaneously, and then, once the curricular teacher is familiar with it, it can also be used when the specialized teacher is not working in the class. In ideal conditions, the curricular teacher attends to the three groups where the child with special needs is not included, or attends to the group where this child is integrated in alternation with the support teacher. Having acquired experience, the curricular teacher will achieve the ability to follow all four groups at once. When this happens it represents a real success, since it also allows work in a satisfactory way when the support teacher is not present.

Secondly, any individual work with the child with difficulties, carried out in short sessions inside, or occasionally, outside the classroom, assumes a different meaning as a reflection of the different atmosphere in the class: since there are times when the whole class works together and times when the work is in small groups or individual, this last condition will be less likely to be perceived as only for people with learning difficulties.

As for the efficacy of this proposed model, we have at present the results of some early research (Vianello, 1990a). The analysis of data concerning 112 teachers in a municipality of north Italy shows that, when the support teacher works in the same room as the curricular teacher or teachers, there is a better collaboration between teachers, and the curricular teachers both feel more involved in the education of the pupils with learning difficulties and are better able to meet their needs during the absence of the support teacher.

THE EDUCATION OF TEACHERS

In Italy, teachers in pre-schools and primary schools do not have a university degree; they only have a diploma awarded after three or four years' attendance at pedagogic school normally at the age of 17 or 18. The amount of time provided for educational and psychological training is altogether insufficient.

Teachers at junior high school, on the other hand, do have a university degree or an equivalent qualification. However, the great majority of these teachers do not receive an adequate training to teach children with disabilities or even those with less severe learning disorders. As we shall indicate further on, teachers tend to make up for the lack of education by taking part in initiatives of in-service training or in training opportunities, such as conferences, congresses or seminars offered by associations.

A positive trend needs to be highlighted here. Many support teachers, specifically trained for special education, tend to move to regular teaching after between five and ten years' experience. Clearly, classes where these teachers work then have the benefit of a wider competence, not only in the teaching of children with special needs but also in individualized teaching in general.

Recent laws are causing a deep change in teacher training. From now on a university degree will be required in order to teach in any kind of school. The curriculum of studies must include courses specifically concerned with pedagogic, psychological and didactic subjects. We can expect that within two or three years only teachers with university degrees will be accepted in pre-schools and primary schools.

The education of support teachers

Currently the specialization of teachers requires two years of further education, comprising 1300 hours, in a private or public school. The general trend is to favour public schools and the participation of teachers already 'on the roll' (qualified and registered).

In the past, three different specializations were provided: in visual impairment, hearing impairment and physical disability; now support teachers must be specialized in all kinds of disability. In fact, as children with disabilities are integrated in regular classes, a teacher may follow at different times of the same day children who as far as possible attend the same school but who have different kinds of disability. It is likely that not far in the future it will be possible to obtain a specialized qualification only after a university degree and by means of courses organized by a university.

The programmes of the schools which provide specialization courses are modular and it is not possible to give a synthesis of them; all we can usefully do is present a summary of the basic ideas which underlie the training (Vianello and Bolzonella, 1988):

The *subjects of study* comprise

- *pedagogics*: general pedagogics, methodology and didactics;
- *psychology*: developmental psychology, educational psychology;
- *clinical studies*: clinical treatment of impairments, therapeutic techniques of rehabilitation.

Within these subjects, methodological comparison covers

- *curricular didactics*: linguistic, logical-mathematical, psychomotor-expressive;
- *operative dimension*: methodologies of observation, functional assessment, analysis of interpersonal dynamics, curricular programming, strategies linked to educational technology, organizational integration.

The in-service training of teachers

As we have seen, in a few years all new regular teachers will possess a university degree and all new support teachers will have a specialized qualification awarded by a university. At present, until this comes about, Italian teachers have to complete their education by means of in-service training. For reasons both of legislation and tradition, schools tend to organize in-service training courses at the beginning of and during the school year. These courses are not always up to expectations. Many teachers, though perhaps a minority, are aware of this, and try to make up for it at their own expense, attending conferences, seminars and workshops organized by non-governmental associations. For the last ten years at least the National Coordination of Specialized Teachers and Research on Handicap (CNIS) has played an important role in this regard. However, the initiatives of CNIS reach less than 10 per cent of teachers involved with children having special needs. In order to promote the correct application of the didactic model presented above, adequate in-service training should help the teacher to learn how to:

- propose to the whole class general, polyfunctional topics;
- elaborate an individualized workplan for the pupil with learning difficulties, to be carried out in a social situation;
- collaborate with other colleagues in planning the syllabus for the pupil with learning difficulties;
- be able to organize and manage small groups.

It can easily be seen that the model of this in-service training has to be flexible; some aspects however tend to be constant. The training can be divided into three phases:

The first phase requires at least six sessions. The first will have an introductory function, the following three being dedicated to workshops in small groups of about five teachers each. The ideal situation is to have 20 teachers divided into four groups, as many trainees as the pupils in a class in which a pupil with special needs is integrated. In the first of these sessions each teacher will have to present his or her own case to the colleagues in the group. At the end the group will choose a general and polyfunctional topic, which should be, as far as possible, adapted for all the presented 'cases'. This is easier than one might think because of the generality of the topic to be chosen, for instance 'a season' or 'a means of transport'. The next task, during the same series of three sessions, will be to elaborate a syllabus for the whole class and another one in parallel for the pupil with special needs. The last two sessions of this first phase will be devoted to plenary work in which each group presents the results of the workshop.

These six sessions have a number of objectives: the awakening of the 'richness' the teachers already possess, the socialization of this 'richness', and an increase in the ability to work with other teachers. Particularly important objectives are training in the elaboration of a syllabus useful for all the pupils of the class, and therefore also for the pupil with learning difficulties, and recognizing and operating the various ways of managing work in small groups, with the teachers playing in a certain sense the role of pupils while their role is assumed by the supervisor of the training.

The second phase consists of the application in two or three months by each teacher of what was planned in the first phase, after a more specific elaboration, considering with care the characteristics and needs of the particular class and of the pupil with special needs.

In the third and final phase the teachers can compare in four to six sessions (two or three workshops and two or three plenary sessions) the results reached during the second phase.

Before concluding, we must consider an aspect which we regard as crucial: the ability to organize and manage small groups. On the basis of our experience, but also of scientific research conducted on small groups (for example Smelser, 1981), we have the following suggestions for the role of the leader of a study group. These have been formulated thinking specifically of teachers involved in training that has characteristics similar to the model just described. With some adjustments, the same suggestions can also be useful for group work carried out with children in a class; some further indications about leading a small group of schoolchildren have already been given in this chapter. Our recommendations for group leaders are as follows:

- Give priority to the reporting of experience, inviting the teachers to specify the aims, the modalities and the assessment of results.
- Invite them to consider what they have learned from their failures, avoiding situations in which teachers are encouraged only to report on successful experiences.
- At the conclusion of a report, invite the teacher to express an opinion about which aspects of his or her experience are also valid for teachers in other situations, after this throwing the question open to the other members of the group.
- Whenever possible, encourage comparisons between various ways of conducting the group.
- Often adopt the practice of inviting all the members of the group in turn to express their opinion on the subject.
- Avoid prolonged dialogues between two members of the group, as this can prevent others from contributing.
- Do not let a member become the pivot of discussion, intervening excessively in comparison to other members.
- Do not assume the role of the expert in the subject, but that of one who promotes comparisons of experiences, opinions and so on.
- Avoid long lists of problems or techniques, laying emphasis on going into single aspects more deeply.
- If a member of the group is inexperienced in a subject, invite him or her to formulate hypotheses, underlining however that they are only hypotheses.
- From time to time invite the group to synthesize the content of the discussion, in order to avoid excessive digressions.
- Do not take a stand for or against the reports, but emphasize their positive side by highlighting aspects that are valid in similar situations; establish links with other reports; make a synthesis for the other members. If the report is too long and confusing, invite the reporter to underline the idea, or at most the three ideas he or she thinks the most important, so that those listening are better able to organize what has been presented; and by inviting all the members to express their opinion on the report, highlight the aspect they found most interesting.
- Ensure that the final report of the group does not comprise more than two or three topics (possibly linked), or exceed one or two pages, so that it may be read in 10 to 15 minutes.

We believe it is important to increase the teacher's awareness of the various ways of conducting a small group. It would seem useful that a member of each group, other than the one reporting on the content of the work, should prepare a report focusing on ways of leading and working. All these reports will be analysed and discussed in the last phase of evaluation of the work done.

REFERENCES

Bernath, K. and Kayser, M. (1991) *Special Education in Switzerland. A General Overview.* Zürich: Pro Infirmis.

Breur, A.J. and Breur de Ru, J. (1989) 'L'integrazione scolastica in Europa: L'Olanda.' In C. Cornoldi and R. Vianello (eds) *Handicap, Memoria e Apprendimento.* Bergamo: Juvenilia.

Cornoldi, C. (1991) *I Disturbi di Apprendimento.* Bologna: Il Mulino.

Da Fonseca, V. (1991) 'Assessment and treatment of learning disabilities in Portugal'. Paper delivered at the 9th International Congress of CNIS, Foggia.

Danielson, D. and Bellamy, G.T. (1988) 'State variation in placement of children with handicaps in segregated environments'. Unpublished paper.

EASE (1991) 'Teacher training in Holland'. *Information from the European Association for Special Education,* **1**, 31–2 (various authors).

Filippini Steinemann, C. (1991) 'L'Integrazione scolastica in Europa: la Svizzera'. *Notiziario CNIS,* **2**, 5–8.

Gugelmann, A. (1989) 'L'Integrazione scolastica in Europa: la Svizzera'. In C. Cornoldi and R. Vianello (eds) *Handicap, Memoria e Apprendimento.* Bergamo: Juvenilia.

Helimäki, L. (1991) 'Special education for the handicapped in Finland: vocational education'. *Information from the European Association for Special Education,* **1**, 24–5.

Jacobsen, P.E. (1989) 'L'Integrazione scolastica in Europa: la Danimarca'. In C. Cornoldi and R. Vianello (eds) *Handicap, Memoria e Apprendimento.* Bergamo: Juvenilia.

Lamoral, P. (1991) 'Assessment and treatment of learning disabilities in Belgium'. Paper delivered at the 9th International Congress of CNIS, Foggia.

Larrivee, B. and Cook, L. (1979) 'Mainstreaming: a study of the variables affecting teacher attitude'. *Journal of Special Education,* **13**, 315–24.

Mittler, P. (1988) 'Special education in Britain'. Paper delivered at the Conference of the Japanese Association for Special Education, September.

Mittler, P. and Farrell, P. (1987) 'Can children with severe learning difficulties be educated in ordinary schools?' *European Journal of Special Needs Education,* **2**(4), 221–36.

Netherlands Ministry of Education and Science (1989) *Special Education in the Netherlands.* Amsterdam.

Østli, A. (1990) 'Reform programme for the mentally retarded in Norway'. *Information from the European Association for Special Education,* **90**(2), 21–2.

Østli, A. (1991) 'L'Integrazione scolastica in Europea: la Norvegia'. In C. Cornoldi and R. Vianello (eds) *Handicap, Memoria e Apprendimento.* Bergamo: Juvenilia.

Preuss, E. (1990) 'Integration in the Federal Republic of Germany'. *Information from the European Association for Special Education,* **2**, 29–30.

Rosenqvist, J. (in press) *The Situation of Integration in Sweden.*

Smelser, N.J. (1981) *Sociology.* Englewood Cliffs, NJ: Prentice-Hall.

Stasinos, D. (1991) 'Assessment and treatment of learning disabilities in Greece'. Paper delivered at the 9th International Congress of CNIS, Foggia.

US Department of Education (1988) *To Assure the Free Appropriate Public Education of All Handicapped Children: Tenth Annual Report to Congress on the Implementation of the Education of the Handicapped Act.* Washington DC: US Department of Education.

Vianello, R. (1988) 'Gli atteggiamenti dei genitori e degli insegnanti nei confronti del minore con insufficienza mentale'. In G. Tampieri, S. Soresi and R. Vianello (eds) *Ritardo Mentale. Rassegna di Ricerche.* Pordenone: ERIP.

Vianello, R. (1989a) 'Attitude of teachers, with or without specific experience, towards educable mentally or physically handicapped pupils'. In R.C. King and J.K. Collins (eds) *Social Applications and Issues in Psychology.* North Holland: Elsevier Science Publishers.

Vianello, R. (1989b) 'L'Integrazione scolastica in Europa: l'Italia'. In C. Cornoldi and R. Vianello (eds) *Handicap, Memoria e Apprendimento*. Bergamo: Juvenilia.

Vianello, R. (1990a) *L'Adolescente con Handicap Mentale e la sua Integrazione Scolastica* Padua: Liviana.

Vianello, R. (1990b) 'Atteggiamenti di adulti e coetanei nei confronti dell'adolescente con handicap mentale'. *Sì Rivista di studi sociali del Veneto*, **6**, 19–57.

Vianello, R. (1992) 'L'Integrazione scolastica degli alunni con handicap in Italia, in Europa, e negli USA: alcune tendenze a confronto'. In M.G. Chiapedi, L. Parmigiani and C. Silvano (eds) *Handicap. La Collaborazione degli Operatori tra Diagnosi Funzionale e Piano Educativo Individualizzato*. Bergamo: Juvenilia.

Vianello, R. (1994) *Psicologia, Sviluppo, Educazione*. Milan: Juvenilia.

Vianello, R. and Bolzonella, G.F. (1988) *Il Bambino Portatore di Handicap e la sua Integrazione Scolastica*. Milan: Juvenilia.

Vianello, R. and Moniga, S. (1994) 'Handicap mentale'. In S. Bonino (ed.) *Dizionario di Psicologia dello Sviluppo*. Turin: Einaudi.

Vitello, S.J. (1989) 'Integration of handicapped students in the United States and Italy: a comparison'. *International Journal of Special Education*, **4**(1), 10–12.

Wenz, K. (1991) 'L'integrazione scolastica in Europa: il Baden-Württemberg'. In R. Vianello and C. Cornoldi (eds) *Stili di Insegnamento, Stili di Apprendimento, Handicap*. Bergamo: Juvenilia.

Chapter 7

Teacher Training and the Integration of Children with Special Needs: Romanian Initiatives

Radu Diaconescu, Miron Ionescu, Vasile Chiş and Patrick Daunt

THE TRAINING OF SPECIAL EDUCATION TEACHERS IN ROMANIA

Initial education

Special education teachers were trained by means of four-year courses in the university faculties of special psychopedagogy until 1972, when the former government prohibited this kind of education. Graduates of this form of teacher education had been employed in the network of special education either as special education teachers (called in Romania 'defectologues' or 'psychopedagogues') or as speech therapists ('logopeds').

The speech therapists, of whom there were only a few, were employed in special schools, regular schools and other educational or health services for children.

Psychopedagogues were employed only in basic education in the special schools (the Romanian term is 'helping school', *Şcoala Ajutatore*), that is, in the special kindergarten (for children aged from 3 to 6 or 7 years) and the first four classes of the primary level. Education in the fifth to eighth classes of the special schools was mainly provided by regular teachers with no background in special education.

Regular schoolteachers were trained at universities in special subjects (biology, chemistry, mathematics and so on); a very small part of the academic curriculum, some 7 to 10.5 per cent, was devoted to general psychology, general pedagogy and teaching methodology, including practical training which took place only in regular schools. Being totally unprepared for special education by their initial professional training programme, these teachers found their first contact with children having special needs a somewhat dramatic experience. We have seen colleagues stressed and crying in front of children with disabilities, because of their lack of appropriate initial training.

These teachers were obliged by the demands of their professional life to acquire some relevant knowledge and skills. No one within the institutional system was interested in training them in special needs education; in-service teacher training was offered in the same framework as for regular teachers even to teachers working in special education. Some teachers succeeded in adapting empirically to the needs of special children, but others became a positive danger to them, exhibiting aggressive unprofessional conduct, resorting excessively to punishment or losing an interest in their work.

Owing to the long period of interruption in the training of special education teachers after 1972, from the 1980s onwards special schools were able to employ only a very few psychopedagogues, speech therapists or psychologists and had to rely largely on regular teachers. The drama of the special educational institutions and of the restricted life of children with disabilities on which the media focused after 1989 was caused to a great extent by the lack of specially trained staff in this field.

In-service teacher training

All in-service teacher training was organized and led by a department in the former Ministry of Education. University faculties were required to carry out training tasks in accordance with strict Ministry regulations. There was little scope for local initiative or autonomy.

In practice, all teachers were obliged to follow refresher courses in the form of university lectures. These occupied about 120 hours in total, of which 30 were devoted to psychology, pedagogy and methodology, and the rest (about 90 hours) to the teacher's special subject. As with initial training, the stress was on the subject matter of one or two specialities rather than on the teaching process.

In-service training was provided at three levels:

1. For official recognition as a fully qualified teacher, after three years a teacher needed a good report from the local Inspector of Education as well as success in the examination following the 120-hour course.
2. To obtain the 'second degree' a teacher, not less than five years after official recognition, again needed a good inspector's report and success in an examination after 120 hours of university lectures.
3. After at least another five years, a teacher could obtain the 'first degree' by means of the same process of inspection and study, as well as the presentation of a project or paper on his or her own subject and teaching methodology.

All teachers were obliged to follow in-service programmes in the special subject in which they graduated. The programmes were centred on theory and scientific knowledge, not oriented towards the development of teaching skills. Teachers teaching mathematics, for example, in a special school were included in the same courses as regular mathematics teachers.

Initial teacher training in Romania today

Pedagogic high schools, called in Romania normal schools or pedagogical lycées, offer education to students from the age of 14 or 15 to 19 or 20. Initial teacher education for five years is provided for future teachers either in kindergartens (children aged from 3 to 6 or 7), the first four classes of primary education (children aged from 6 or 7 to 10 or 11), or special schools (the same age-groups as for the primary schools, for educational activities organized after the school programme, usually in the afternoon; formal teaching, usually in the morning, is given by a psychopedagogue).

Universities prepare students in one or two branches of science, arts, culture, technical studies and so on; the students can receive a teaching certificate if they fulfil the requirements of the *Pedagogical Seminar* (see below).

Special faculties in universities also prepare teachers for special education as well as training other specialists, such as psychologists, pedagogues, speech therapists, social workers.

Current developments

At present some important changes have been implemented or are being implemented in the initial and in-service training programmes of both special and regular teachers. New structures have been created for this purpose. The universities have now been given autonomy in initial teacher training and the department for in-service training in the Ministry is now sharing its responsibilities; in the reorganization currently being undertaken, in-service programmes are being developed on a regional basis by three institutions: the Pedagogical Seminar of the university, the educational inspectorate of the county (*Judeţ*) and the Teachers' House (teachers' centre).

The principal changes are these:

- Faculties which provide initial training for professionals to work with children having special needs have resumed their work; leading universities (Bucharest, Cluj, Iasi, Timisoara) have opened faculties or sub-faculties in pedagogy, psychology, psychopedagogy, sociology and social work.
- All initial teacher training is controlled and provided by the Pedagogical Seminar (Seminarul Pedagogic), created by the Ministry of Education in 1993.
- The Pedagogical Seminar is responsible for the certification of teachers. Students who want to be teachers have to fulfil the targets set by the Seminar; this involves a total of 210 hours of study broken down as follows:
  - 28 hours of lectures and 14 hours of seminars on the psychology of education and child development;
  - 56 hours of lectures and 28 hours of seminars on pedagogy and didactics;
  - 28 hours of seminars on the methodology of teaching the student's subject or subjects;
  - about 56 hours of practical exercises in designing lessons, teaching in the classroom and so on.
- Because the University of Cluj has a strong tradition in the field of special education and is well oriented towards integrated education, there are some important elements relating to special needs in the training of regular teachers in the Cluj Seminar. The curriculum for the psychology of education and pedagogy provides for lectures and seminars on special education and study visits in special schools, and priority is also given to providing for practical training in special schools. In addition, the Seminar is developing lectures, workshops and conferences on special needs education with groups of regular teachers.

- The pedagogical lycées responsible for the education of primary teachers have also introduced important themes on the education of children with special needs; a main topic on special education has been introduced in the fourth year.
- In general, the education of teachers and other professionals engaged in special needs is receiving particular attention in Romanian institutions. For example, the four universities just mentioned have agreed to coordinate their special training programmes and are preparing a project to create a master's degree in special education. This follows the establishment of master's degree courses, as a new element in the curriculum of the universities, by Decision 283/93 of the national Ministry. In accordance with the national priorities laid down for the TEMPUS (East–West university cooperation) programme of the European Union, which for 1995–6 include the creation of master's degrees in (among other areas) the humanities, the four universities are exploring the possibility of developing a joint European project for this purpose. This initiative is intended to support the national programme on educational integration (see p. 73).

Priorities for the future

The most important objectives for future teacher training in relation to special needs education are these:

- There is a need for curriculum development in initial training in order to prepare primary and secondary teachers for the new integrated approach.
- This implies the need for retraining trainers both in universities and at the level of the inclusive or integrated school, in order to update their knowledge.
- There is a need for specialized equipment and teaching aids (including for example computers and aids for speech therapy), and more generally for aids to support new methods appropriate to the inclusive classroom.
- There will be a place too for training courses delivered in the universities by trainers from other European countries, in order to develop teaching skills for the benefit of local teaching staff and students.
- There would be great benefit from mobility schemes which enabled undergraduate and postgraduate students to have study periods and practical placements in universities and in inclusive or integrated schools in other European countries.

OTHER DEVELOPMENTS (I): THE NON-GOVERNMENTAL ORGANIZATIONS

In order to set in context the demands of and possibilities for special needs teacher training which have just been outlined, two other important Romanian developments have to be understood. The first is the creation and increasing vitality of a number of voluntary, non-governmental organizations (NGOs) working at national or local level in the field of special needs. The other is the launch by the Ministry of Education in 1993 of a national programme to promote the educational and social integration of children and young people with special needs.

The last decade of this century has brought many new developments in the part played by Romanian NGOs in social activity, as their role has become more important and their programmes recognized and supported by the governments of many European countries. Since 1990 a real explosion of non-governmental programmes and projects, mainly in the social field, has taken place in Romania, originated by numerous NGOs that have come to Romania from all over the world. The first programmes targeted the emergency of that time, as they concerned the most vulnerable groups such as institutions for disabled children, and orphanages.

Many of these projects have been either terminated or restructured in the light of the experience of launching and implementing them. Among the reasons for this have been Romanian realities after the revolution, the involvement of Romanians eager to take action in the social field, the appearance of the first Romanian NGOs, and (on the other hand) the resistance of bureaucratic structures in the institutions and the traditional mentality of many people.

The appearance of the Romanian NGOs has created some at least of the conditions necessary for Romanian citizens to have the independence to act as pressure groups in relation to institutions which kept their isolation for over 50 years of communist dictatorship, and whose officials were reluctant to accept the process of transformation of the individual from a simple listener to a human being with a distinct personality. The new NGOs, although without experience, have brought into play the philosophy of microsocial organizations which aim to represent the specific interests of larger social groups such as children and young people, interests which are often neglected by an inflexible administrative structure, the state still having the predominant role at all levels of economic and social life. This is why a number of projects and programmes, originally designed as crisis interventions and limited to the provision to institutions of food and clothing, started to restructure their activities for the medium and longer term to include not only immediate support but also the development of a human personality appropriate to the spirit of our times. The aim has become that of achieving at least minimal independence for those who are vulnerable, thus facilitating real integration.

Relevant to this development has been the way in which large projects financed by the different foreign NGOs or by the European Union have generated other, smaller projects, which while inspired by the experience of other countries were better adapted to Romanian realities. The Romanian NGOs that promoted these activities began to be important elements in the implementation of reform, able to transmit messages to and from the citizens and the authorities, and, even more importantly, able to establish international contacts and cooperation.

The Experience in County Dolj

Into this context we can set the experience shared between the Danish Red Barnet (Save the Children) and three Romanian NGOs in County Dolj, which is situated in the south of the country between the Carpathian mountains and the Danube, and the chief city of which is Craiova. The three NGOs are the Centre for the Education and Development of the Personality of the Child, the Helios Foundation (not connected directly with the Helios programme of the European Union) and the Hand Int Foundation. Because of its practical approach, Red Barnet was able to establish contacts with a number of different Danish counties, so that specialists from county councils and institutions there could function as professional and managerial leaders for each project within the programme.

One project, aiming at 'Institutional Development and Change', has been carried out by the County of Storstrøm, and has had as manager Mr Henrick Haubro, a psychologist. The main aim of the project has been to develop and change the institutional system, especially the establishments for children with disabilities and the orphanages, in accordance with the principle of normalization. From the start it was agreed that in order to effect change of this kind active involvement of the existing structures was essential: the kindergartens, the vocational schools, the assessment procedures and so on. This was seen to be especially important if the experience was to be replicated in other districts of Romania.

For the implementation of the project the starting point was the theoretical framework derived from the defined objectives, based on the Nordic experience of child care and deinstitutionalization, all this being adapted to the Romanian conditions and in accordance with the United Nations Declaration on Children's Rights and the Declaration of the European Union on the Rights of Disabled People.

Although the Romanian authorities agreed with the project's objectives, practical activities faced some difficulties because of the traditional belief in Romanian society that disabled people, especially those with the more severe disabilities, should be isolated in institutions, that they should in some cases be regarded as 'incurables', and that they should remain invisible to the community. Having these realities, which could not be ignored, in view, the managers of the project chose two strategies for its first phase: to create acceptance and understanding among the key persons, and to direct the work towards the children with the most severe disabilities, in order to make them socially visible and able to learn. This double strategy was necessary for two reasons. For one thing, the time scale of the project was rather short for the attainment of sustainable change. Secondly, it was essential to win over the staff of the institutions and public opinion by enabling them to see that change could be sustained and accepted, and that the so-called incurable children are able to learn and deserve affection.

Practical implementation of the project began with a process of review. As a result of this, it was decided, with the agreement of the Romanian authorities, to change the living conditions of the children in the psychiatric hospital at Poiana Mare and the residential hospital at Corlate. In cooperation with the County Dolj Inspectorate for the Handicapped, 168 children were transferred from these two institutions, and were placed in special schools, in a new residential hospital and in two towns in Dolj. At the same time, two community-based group homes were established by the purchase (with the aid of foreign resources) of two buildings, which were donated to the Romanian authorities.

The difficulty which Red Barnet sometimes experienced in understanding the Romanian realities, the replacement of managers sympathetic to change by others more resistant to it, the financial situation of the Romanian authorities, as well as Red Barnet's decision to discontinue funding of the group homes – all these factors determined the leaders of the project to start looking for additional solutions, in order to ensure positive evolution of their achievements.

In agreement with development groups of Romanian specialists who were cooperating with the project, three NGOs were established, which received substantial support from Storstrøm County in Denmark and from the province of Álava in the Spanish Basque country. These three NGOs were, in chronological order, the Centre for the Education and Development of the Child (CEDCP), the Hand Int Foundation and the Helios Foundation. Having their own juridical status, each has established its own distinct objectives, but together they have been able to continue the process started by the project.

With this aim in view, the Helios Foundation, with financial support from Álava province, has bought a house and two apartments and signed a convention with the Romanian authorities for the decentralized care of young people with intellectual or psychological disabilities. At present, 27 young people are being cared for in these group homes, which, together with the 24 children in houses under the authority of the institutions, makes a total of 51 children and young people with disabilities living in family-like conditions.

The Hand Int organization, in accordance with the aims laid down in a legal document creating a trading company, Orizont Int Hand, has as its main purpose the vocational integration of young people with disabilities. By opening a tailoring workshop where most employees are disabled, this company has succeeded in offering a working position to a number of young people with disabilities, on a small scale at first, but with the potential to develop the service area so as to create a higher number of work places for this category of young people. The highly creative workshops established by the Helios Foundation, also offering work to a number of teenagers with disabilities, have raised the number of disabled young people employed by two NGOs alone to 32.

It must also be said that cooperation with the institutions has given results. This has arisen from local initiatives, as a result of direct discussions with the institutions and with the support of the local authorities. It has largely related to integration in the educational system. The problems of the young people from Poiana Mare and Corlate were very special owing to their status as 'incurables' in the two hospitals, where there were no educational facilities. Through an agreement with the Inspectorate for Education and the Inspectorate for the Handicapped, the children of school age from the group home known as the Lego House have been able to attend a special school as day pupils just like any child living in a family. The children from the Calaminești House have been included in a programme of educational rehabilitation and social integration by the director of the Matei Basarab High School, who is also a founder member of CEDCP.

The problem to be solved was that these young people from Calimanești House were illiterate and over school age according to Romanian law. For this reason it was decided that they should be trained in a workshop producing sanitary equipment, without aiming at formal qualification but with the objectives of social integration and the development of skills, responsibility and the capacity for social relationships. In a very short time, it could be seen that their integration into a society of normal young people did not cause any problems; the others regarded them as colleagues whom they should help to learn, and not at all as handicapped persons. The progress made by the young people with disabilities was surprisingly fast. Their social behaviour soon changed, and people who did not know them could not tell the difference between them and their normal colleagues.

Finally, there was the need to inform the public about all these activities in order both to obtain general support for them and to make a contribution to the creation of a civil society that is able to decide consciously whether to welcome and support these activities or not, rather than to accept them in the manner of the old obedient society.

For this purpose, the third NGO, the Centre for the Education and Development of the Personality of the Child started its activity. This was based on the objectives set out in its statute, to influence public opinion for the benefit of children and young people, without discrimination, by means of five functions: information; documentation; instruction and education; programmes for children; and practical support for these programmes. The programmes implemented by the CEDCP have aimed at using modern means for informing the public about these vulnerable children and young people. Groups of children and young people without disabilities involved in the Centre's programme of free expression willingly agreed to cooperate with those from the group homes in the production of information. A series of brochures and folders was edited which reflected the new conditions of the children's lives in the decentralized institutions. The first success with this material was a brochure of texts and pictures called *Our Homes*. This was a way of putting into practice the principle of equal value: the children with disabilities were no longer sensational subjects but were perceived as participating in the editing of a brochure about themselves on an equal footing with the others.

This idea of a brochure was later developed in making films about these experiences. The three films about the group homes benefited from the direct participation of the young people from the Calimaneşti House and used some of their ideas; some of the young people participated directly in making the films with the team, the others being actors or responsible for sound effects. Those running the Centre have observed their joy when they saw the films, and their eagerness to show them to other friends and guests.

By taking seriously the activity of informing public opinion, with the aim of changing old mentalities and making visible the positive aspects of the personalities of these children who had been considered a burden on society, the Centre has succeeded in convincing the media of the importance of this information. The moment the video studio produces films and documentaries for a local television channel, the Centre obtains the cooperation of the regional radio station on which the children can participate directly with shows produced by themselves. It also edits magazines made entirely by the children.

The Centre, in cooperation with Storstrøm County, has succeeded in initiating two seminars on the importance of public information in the education of individual people for a civil society, seminars that brought together the most important institutions dealing with information in our district: the Inspectorate for Education, the Inspectorate for Culture, the libraries, the local newspaper and the local television station. The next important project that the Centre hopes to put into practice is an FM radio station for children and young people, one that could cover a large part of the information for this section of society, enabling them to come up to the level of their age rather than remaining a marginalized group, as has happened to disabled children and young people in the past. Moreover, the joint venture of the specialists from Storstrøm County and the Romanian NGOs has had as a main strategy this large-scale involvement of disabled and normal children together.

In summary, it should be noted that of the 168 children and young people transferred from the two institutions, over half (89) have been integrated into the educational system and are enjoying an educational process which is already showing positive results.

The relevance of the NGOs to teacher training

The experience in County Dolj is one of many examples of the development of Romanian NGOs from or in association with a foreign initiative which may be found in all quarters of the country. Others are Noi de Asemenea ('We're all alike') in Piatra Neamţ in Moldavia, which derives from an initiative of the Swiss Médecins sans Frontières and which is promoting the integration in neighbourhood schools of children from a large local orphanage, as well as working on the problems of early postnatal care and of street children; Centrul de Zi in Bucharest, a day centre for children with severe learning difficulties, supported by East European Partnership; Speranţa in Timişoara, which offers therapy for severely physically disabled children and remedial services to children with mild or moderate learning difficulties; the Primavara rehabilitation centre in Reşitsa in County Caraş-Severin, supported by Norwegian People's Aid; and Aras in Constanţa, whose fundamental work with children infected with HIV is supported by World Vision.

Also important is the development of national associations, which are often inspired and run by parents of children with disabilities; some of these have acquired branches throughout the country and large memberships. They include the Association for the Support of People with Mental Handicaps, based in Cluj; the Association for the Neuromotor Handicapped of Romania, based in Arad; and the Romanian Association for Persons with Mental Handicap and the Association for the Support of Physically Handicapped Children, both with headquarters in Bucharest. The existence and activities of these and other similar NGOs have profound implications for the whole future of education in Romania, and of special needs education in particular, and for the training both of regular and specialized teachers.

By forming the vanguard of the movement to promote an 'open society' and a 'civil society' in Romania, the NGOs are changing attitudes, setting up lines of communication and enabling exchanges of information and opinion which simply have not existed for a generation at the least. In particular, they are bringing about a revolution in the relationship between the families and the 'system', by which is meant not only the Ministry and its representatives (the Inspectorate) but also the training institutions (universities and pedagogic high schools) and the special primary and secondary schools themselves. The beginning of a completely new form of accountability of the institutions towards the children and their families can be perceived, as well as the proliferation of diverse activities and communications in which professionals and families are for the first time jointly involved, and which in themselves constitute invaluable training provision, informal but radical.

Operating both as pressure groups and as providers of innovatory services, the NGOs have the potential both to change attitudes by direct influence and to set up practices which will change attitudes still further. For the providers of formal teacher training they constitute both a new challenge and a new source of invaluable support.

OTHER DEVELOPMENTS (2): THE NATIONAL INTEGRATION PROGRAMME

In 1991, with the sponsorship of UNICEF and UNESCO, the Romanian authorities organized a first national professional conference in Bucharest to review the system of special education. It was agreed that the time had come to progress beyond the elimination of intolerable living conditions to a general improvement in the quality of education provided (Tatoiu, 1994). While there were some reservations, considerable interest was shown in the concepts of integration and normalization. The three foreign consultants attending the conference under UNESCO's auspices prepared a draft proposal for the setting up of nationally coordinated but locally based pilot projects to promote the educational and social integration of children and young people with disabilities of whatever kind or severity.

By the beginning of 1993 the Romanian Ministry was in a position to accept the proposal, and after a period of careful preparation two such projects, in the cities of Cluj and Timişoara, were launched in October of that year. UNESCO has continued to provide political, moral and technical support and UNICEF has in addition provided funds without which the whole initiative would have been impossible.

Since then the two projects have worked closely together. Both project teams are led by directors of schools engaged in mainstreaming, the one in Timişoara being head of a general (7–16 years) school in which children with various disabilities are individually mainstreamed, the Cluj leader being head of a special school which has established and staffed a special unit in a neighbouring general school. The projects, which will run for three years, presented their interim reports in 1995. The activities of the first 18 months have been concentrated on the preparation and implementation of further individual placements in the general schools, the creation of integrated kindergartens, the provision of special school places for children with severe physical disabilities previously denied formal education, the development of integrated leisure activities for children and young people and cooperation with the local media. Considerable priority has been given to semi-formal training sessions for teachers, other professionals and parents; intensive courses have also been delivered by consultants from the Universities of Malaga and London (Institute of Education), who are also offering evaluation services to the projects.

Since the projects were launched there have been three important developments in the conception of the programme (Vrasmaş and Daunt, 1994). The first has been the initiation of a strategy for the dissemination and generalization of the experience of the pilot projects and of the notion of integration by means of a regional plan which will give outreach to all the counties of the country. The second has been the adoption of a 'holistic' view of integration: development led rather than doctrine led. This approach implies the recognition that all institutions and groups have a possible integration plan which is realistic and that all actions which improve the quality of life and of education of children 'in the here and now' are equally valid (all right actions are equally good) and therefore to be equally valued. Implied in turn is the abandonment of the term 'levels of integration', since this implies a hierarchy of values among actions, and so eventually among the children involved: that is a direct infraction of the equal-value principle, so one must speak only of different 'forms' and 'kinds' of integration. The programme is engaged in establishing an authentically Romanian taxonomy of integration on these lines.

The third development has been the extension of the programme from one component (the pilot projects) to three, all interdependent. Of the new elements, one is the activity of East–West university cooperation mentioned earlier in this chapter. It is obvious that the changes being considered and already implemented have radical implications for both initial and in-service training; indeed the Ministry's aims cannot be achieved without significant curriculum development in the education of teachers. At the same time the pilot projects offer both a stimulus and a test-bed for those university departments already committed to taking a lead in reform. In the future, the strongly regional character of the mission of the universities will encourage them to contribute actively to the process of regional generalization.

The other added element has been the creation of a national information, communication and cooperation network of associations, institutions, centres and projects engaged in promoting educational or social integration. The Network, formally launched with about thirty members in Bucharest in the early summer of 1993, had its first conference in Piatra Neamţ in Moldavia that autumn, where agreement was reached on the services which the Network would offer to its membership and a philosophy of equality of all the members established. Already the Network has ensured a forum for quite new forms of open dialogue between the NGOs and the institutions, and it too will have a vital part to play in the generalization process.

Summary

It can be hoped that the three interactive elements of the Romanian Ministry of Education's national integration programme, provided no one of them falters, will together ensure the initiation and dissemination of both formal and informal activities in the training of teachers, other professionals and family members, of a quality and ubiquity commensurate with the aspirations and potential of children with special needs, the reality of which is now so widely recognized in Romanian society.

REFERENCES

Tatoiu, M.S. (1994) 'Special education in Romania'. *European Journal of Special Needs Education*, **9**(3), 236–45.
Vrasmaş, T. and Daunt, P.E. (1994) 'The Romanian National Programme to promote the educational and social integration of children and young people with special needs.' Paper presented at the 6th European Regional Conference of Rehabilitation International, Budapest, 4–9 September.

Chapter 8

East–West Cooperation for Pupils with SEN: A Report on a TEMPUS Project

Mike Johnson

To quote a famous first sentence: 'It was the best of times, it was the worst of times.'

> *Messages from Lithuania: 'Your fax has arrived at the Ministry – the Minister has resigned.' 'Your hotel has hot water – at weekends.'*

> *This is your Captain speaking: 'We will soon be departing for Lithuania – when we can get one of the engines started.'*

Thus in September 1992 began the TEMPUS project mounted by the Manchester Metropolitan University (MMU), as contractor and coordinator, the Institut Universitaire de la Formation des Maîtres (IUFM) Grenoble, as European Union partner and the Siauliai Pedagogical Institute from the 'eligible country'. TEMPUS (Trans European Mobility Programme for University Staff) is a small part of the PHARE (Poland and Hungary Aid to Restore the Economy) initiative. The Baltic states became part of that scheme rather than the scheme for the CIS and its former satellites (TACIS) as their incorporation into the USSR was not formally accepted by the West. It provides money for inter-university cooperation in the restructuring and developing of courses and curricula with the ultimate aim of producing economic gains in the eligible country. The funds can be used for 'mobility' to allow for teaching in and 'missions' to the eligible country by tutors from EU universities and visits and 'practical placements' by tutors from that country to the EU. They may also be used to pay for replacement of the time spent on the project by tutors in all the cooperating universities. There are also funds for the administrative support of the project and for coordination meetings. Half the funds allocated must be spent on equipment for the benefit of the eligible country. Projects must aim to produce economic gains for the eligible country and as wide an enhancement of facilities in the eligible country as possible. The firm, overarching criterion is that all activities must be for the direct benefit of the tutors at the partner university in the 'eligible country'. The amounts involved have risen from 25 million ECU in 1990–91 to 193 million ECU in 1993–94. In 1990–91 153 universities were involved, 637 in 1992–93 and 1784 in 1994. There have been 12,212 student and 18,000 staff mobilities. The UK participates in 52 per cent of the activities, has 23 per cent of the contracts and coordinates a further 15 per cent.

Our contract and cooperation are with the Siauliai Pedagogical Institute in the Republic of Lithuania. Lithuania, the southernmost of the Baltic states, is predominantly rural and agricultural. There are a few large towns and many quite isolated settlements. Communications are reliable if somewhat slow and there is a very strong sense of community and culture that is nationalistic not xenophobic. The area is 25,000 square miles and the population 3.5 million: 80 per cent are ethnic Lithuanians, the remainder Poles, Ukrainians, Belorussians and Jews who have been there for many generations. There are also the remains of the occupying Soviets who currently are having to choose whether to become naturalized Lithuanians. There are many scare stories being circulated about this, though it seems to be causing less of a problem than in Estonia and Latvia.

The education system is based on the 'ten-year-comprehensive' model from the ages of 6 to 16. The schools in the towns can be large. Mokykla 21 which, with a school for 'speech pathology', is our centre of excellence for the integration of pupils with special educational needs (SEN) has 2000 pupils, of whom 1000 are in the junior department. There is a good supply of pre-school and nursery provision including special nurseries for pupils with SEN. There are separate schools, some residential, for pupils with moderate learning difficulties (MLD), speech pathology (perhaps the same as communication problems), physical disabilities, scoliosis, and visual and hearing disabilities. There are also residential schools for 'social orphans'. These are for children whose parents are alcoholics, drug abusers or criminals. Such parents were seen by the Soviet occupiers as having forfeited the right to bring up children, a practice which seems to have convinced mainstream schoolteachers very firmly that the reasons for school failure lie outside the school.

Whilst we could see little educational or other justification for having most of these pupils in a residential setting they showed few signs of institutionalization. Granted they slept in dormitories, had their meals in a refectory and were served by a full staff of cleaners and carers. Nevertheless great efforts were made to give them access to the local community and they looked well cared for in every way and were just as lively and inquisitive as any other pupils of their age. One of the statements we have made most clearly to all the officials is that before such schools are closed arrangements must be made for a similar quality of care to be available in the community.

Pupils with severe learning difficulties (SLD) have just entered the educational system. Previously they lived in the 'house of hope', had little, if any, education and officially did not exist. Their carers were paid much less than the normal rate, and there was little if any training in this area. Children with profound and multiple learning difficulties (PMLD) were in residential homes (hospitals) with care workers, again with little or no training and no curriculum to work to. Pupils with emotional and behavioural difficulties (EBD; social delinquents) had been the best hidden in residential schools. We have made contact with one such school, Grusdsidi, 40 kilometres outside Siauliai. Again, their teachers and carers were dedicated but with little training and needing curriculum development.

The teacher training associated with this structure currently takes four or five years full time, but this is changing as a result of the project. Most of the students come straight from school and can choose to take a mainstream or a special needs course. If they wish to become logopaedists (speech therapists) they stay on for an extra year. The courses start at 8.30 a.m. and go on to 4.30 p.m., with few breaks and little time for personal study or reading. This, in any case, would be difficult as there is a great shortage of books. The library is based on the same principle as the British Library: one goes to a hatch, presents a slip with the title of the book one requires and this is then issued, if available. Most sessions are of lecture format, and because of the lack of written material students take careful notes for the examinations. The curriculum is very theoretical, with units in psychology, pedagogy, the history of education and so on along with curriculum subject didactics. The students are all expected to learn folk singing and dancing as part of the cultural transmission element of education. In-service courses are available but again are very theoretical in orientation.

The schools are formal in their teaching, with pupils sitting in rows and working from textbooks. Their work is similarly formal, with 'recitation' being a common lesson format. Here the teacher 'recites' a carefully prepared lesson. The pupils study this at home and come the next day ready to 'recite' to the class on demand. The written work involves either filling in gaps in books, performing mechanical calculations or writing. Pupils with SEN tend to have other, simplified textbooks where they tick off the answers or fill in the words rather than writing; one of the first questions we were asked was what our textbooks would look like. Reports are made to parents on a 10-point scale each week. Learning difficulties were seen by the teachers we met to come mainly from some form of brain damage, parental drunkenness or both.

A major survey of the attitudes of teachers in the Siauliai schools towards SEN was undertaken, involving collection of:

- factual data about the school and its teachers and other workers;
- definitions of SEN currently held by the head and teachers of the school;
- descriptions of pupils thought to have SEN, followed by detailed questions about how they were identified, what are the manifestations of SEN, how they are helped and so on.

Questionnaires were sent to 22 12-year schools, two 9-year schools and two primary schools. Altogether about 1800 teachers and others are involved. The data are now in and being processed. Preliminary indications confirm the impression that factors within the child and/or his family are seen as the main determinants of SEN, and that professional intervention is required.

A further piece of work with the 1000 pupils and 39 teachers in the Mokykla 21 lower school, using Fraser's 'My Class Inventory', produced complementary evidence (Johnson and Martineniene, 1994). This is quite a short inventory, asking both pupils and their teachers about the quality of classroom life they currently experience and would prefer. It was interesting that the inventory transferred directly to the Lithuanian context. Fraser's dimensions of 'satisfaction', 'competition', 'cohesion', 'friction' and 'difficulty' were shown to be meaningful to Lithuanian teachers and pupils. Both groups were agreed that there were high levels of satisfaction and competition, moderately high cohesion and lower levels of friction and difficulty. The pupils believe that the work they are given is more difficult than do the teachers. The teachers agree that it should be easier, and both groups would want to lower it by approximately the same amount. This of course means that the absolute level claimed to be preferred by the teachers is lower than that of the pupils. It would be interesting to follow this up by seeking teachers' and pupils' perceptions of the sources of difficulty. On the face of it one would expect the teachers to be in control of the difficulty of the material presented to their pupils but they do not seem to feel that this is the case in practice.

It is also interesting that, if anything, the pupils' views of preferred difficulty are more realistic than those of the teachers. Low levels of scale score could result in unstimulating, boring work unless the sources of difficulty lie in the methods of curriculum presentation rather than content. Turning to the four affective dimensions, the greatest levels of difference between 'actual' and 'preferred' levels for both pupils and teachers are on competition and friction. There is good agreement between teachers and pupils on the actual and preferred levels of both, but the teachers would reduce them by slightly more than the pupils. This was seen as a fruitful area of intervention.

Some interesting differences between year groups emerged. Teachers in year 1 are satisfied that the level of friction they perceive in their classes is acceptable. The pupils clearly are not. Year 2 teachers also reject the levels of friction they find whilst the year 2 pupils report the difference between actual and perceived friction as basically unchanged. Our hypothesis is that year 1 teachers see the perceived friction as a function of beginning school. Young children are thought to be coming to terms with being in close contact with each other for protracted periods. The expectation is that 'they will grow out of it'. Clearly they do not. The year 2 teachers may believe that year 1 teachers should ensure that pupils are socialized into the school situation and find the levels of bickering, mutual teasing and impatience with others unacceptable.

The range of responses in each class was indicated by the standard deviation for the scale scores. The larger the standard deviation the greater degree of disagreement *within* the class about the actual or preferred level of the characteristic. Eleven classes showed large disagreements on actual coherence, five of them in year 3. Eight show disagreement on preferred competition, seven in year 3. Clearly year 3 pupils see the situation in their classes quite differently from each other where these two factors are concerned. Does the 'actual coherence' data mean that there are exclusive groups forming who experience good coherence amongst themselves but reject other pupils? Are there some who thrive on competition because they have learned how to succeed?

This research is an example of one of our approaches stemming from the concept of dilemmas. The Siauliai Pedagogical Institute (SPI) tutors and the school were presented with a simple method of investigating classroom dynamics. The results can be used directly to facilitate negotiation between teacher and pupil and have clear in-service implications. Those implications were addressed during a visit when courses were offered on classroom management using, amongst other techniques, 'Circle Time' (Mosley, 1993). Teachers were offered knowledge and skills in order to enchance their ability to offer effective education to *all* the pupils in their classes. This reduces the dilemma of feeling that a desirable change from one point of view is undesirable from another. Integration is now more acceptable because it is perceived as leading to greater effectiveness rather than threatening current levels of competence. Teachers quite rightly demand more 'resources' if they are to be responsible for a wider spectrum of pupils. However, such resources need to be seen as personal and professional rather than merely material.

The prime aim of the project is the development of teacher education courses at the SPI so as to increase the proportion of pupils with SEN taught in mainstream settings and reduce the numbers in residential institutions. Economic gains are projected to come from the closure of those institutions and the redeployment of their teaching staff into mainstream settings and their care staff into community-based homes or services. Further gains will come from the greater likelihood of the employment of the pupils and students through their greater integration into the normal life of the community, and therefore their acceptance by that community as potential workers.

During the project the complexity of the undertaking and its inevitable ramifications have become increasingly apparent. Colleagues from other parts of the Faculty have become involved in the initiation of courses for the staff of the new social services. I have supported staff and service development at the Republican Diagnostic Centre which assesses pupils thought to have SEN, and written proposals for its closer association with the Schools' Psychological Service. We have been the first English visitors to schools in rural communities, an institution for 'social delinquents' and the 'houses of hope' for pupils with severe learning difficulties. We have 'found' the pupils with PMLD and EBD. However, this chapter will confine itself to the teacher education facet of the project.

With the taking of freedom in 1991 and the consequent opening of borders there had been a marked increase in the number of visitors from Western countries to the Baltic states. Many of them seemed to have firmly rooted preconceptions. One group had reported back to the Ministry that the whole education system needed scrapping. Another had presented a long list of bad practices. It is somewhat humbling to have a senior official at the Ministry say, 'Tell us what *you* think – we can't be doing everything wrong, can we?' Whilst we were concerned not to be seen to have solutions to be imposed, equally it is not supportive to suggest that we had nothing to offer, and so the philosophy of the project is based on the principle that all those potentially affected by changes should have a voice and, if possible, an involvement in the events leading to such changes. The work is based on the social psychology of 'dilemmas', in particular ideological dilemmas (Billig *et al.*, 1988), especially as related to SEN by Norwich (1993).

The application of the theory to various national situations in Fulcher (1989) was an illuminating source of understandings. Application of this principle enhances the likelihood that any resulting structures and processes will be Lithuanian in character because they have been derived by Lithuanians. Our experiences over the past three years have confirmed an initial concern that a major danger to any such project was an inherent power imbalance between that 'eligible country' and the EU partners. This concern came originally from professional involvement with special educational needs. Here one is constantly faced with the dilemmas created by situations containing a perceived or actual imbalance of power or knowledge: for example, between teachers and parents, doctors, psychologists or other professionals and teachers, between therapy and education, between the needs of pupils and the limits of resources. Special education also provides many examples of the results for pupils of the single-minded application of a theory or set of assumptions in schools in both Western and Eastern Europe. Such situations are again examples of power imbalance, where it is assumed that one group has access to theoretical foundations that are not available to the other, and therefore subservient, group. In a post-communist situation this is given added weight.

Good examples in the UK are the current debates about how to teach reading, the content of the curriculum for 'non-academic' pupils and the meaning of National

Curriculum subjects for pupils with severe learning difficulties. Much practice is based either on partly understood theory or on inertial continuation of standard practice. As there is no alternative provision or source of critique, only the 'happiness test' is applied. I have examined this subject in detail in the proceedings of the SPI International Conference of January 1994 (Johnson, 1994). It was also examined at the Vilnius conference on psychology and pedagogy in teacher education in June 1994 (Johnson, 1995).

The methods by which the philosophy was to be articulated were those of:

–   sharing with our SPI colleagues best practice in both the UK and France in schools and teacher training;
–   sharing with our SPI colleagues the personal theories and philosophies of the teachers and lecturers involved;
–   supporting a centre of excellence in a mainstream school and a centre of expertise in a special school where the staff were encouraged to develop their own 'practice-based theory' and to publicize the results;
–   linking with any national, regional or local services or structures relating to pupils with SEN.

The mechanisms for the delivery of the project were seen as:

–   mobility to the UK by teams of tutors from the Special Educational Needs Faculty of the SPI to visit schools, teachers' centres and the MMU to gain experience of supported integration and of the initial and in-service teacher education courses and LEA structures associated with it;
–   collaboration with the project team at the SPI in the setting up of new courses for teacher education at both initial and in-service levels;
–   the development of an integrated 'centre of excellence' in Mokykla 21 and a 'centre of expertise' in the residential school at Venta;
–   maximal publicity of the results of the project in the Republic. Both the institute and the centres would welcome visitors to learn in detail what was being done.

These methods accept not only that all concerned have a set of personal, professional and political dilemmas in relation to their work, but also that these dilemmas are ideological in nature and that those involved are, at least in part, aware of them. As with Kelly's constructs (or possibly, though perhaps cynically, Maslow's needs) it is likely that such dilemmas are hierarchical in nature. The recent coming of freedom for Lithuania has been a powerful force which has restructured hierarchies, and the ambivalent results of this for the lives of ordinary people are clear. For example there has been a major decline in the health of the general population over the past five years in all the countries previously under Soviet influence. There is no way of knowing how the economic or political situation will develop; our methods therefore must aim to act on at least two levels, enabling individuals both to reach a new *rapprochement* with their own dilemmas and to be willing and able to recognize and accept the same process in others.

This goes against the structures and assumptions currently underlying the approach to SEN in Lithuania. These are stated in what Fulcher (1989) describes as the 'professional discourse'. One hears much of what she calls 'medical discourse, disability discourse and charity discourse'. Individual difficulties are described in terms of personal defects, generalized into syndromes and requiring to be 'diagnosed' and subjected to treatment by a professional. Pupils with difficulties are to be taken very good care of because they engender sympathy and are in need of help. Unfortunately, as Norwich (1993) indicates, the downside of this is that there is an accompanying 'lay discourse' which is associated with fear, prejudice and resentment if people with disabilities emerge from their segregated settings and begin to look for a place in the mainstream community.

The alternative to this professionalism is 'democratism'. Here the discourse is a 'rights discourse', stressing equality and self-reliance and opposing discrimination and oppression. The effects of an over-reliance on professional expertise are insidious. When talking to a group of parents of children with spina bifida I outlined a 'respite' model based on 'foster-aunts'. Here families offer overnight or weekend care for pupils with disabilities so that their parents can have an enhanced personal and social life. This was met with incredulity. In Lithuania no one who did not themselves have a child with a disability would 'want to know', I was told. Yet such attitudes are not consistent with the Lithuanian national characteristics of care and support by the local community.

As a result of two years' work we have come to the following conclusions:

1. The project should follow two broad strands for the integration of pupils with SEN into mainstream settings in Lithuania:

    First the integration of children currently only cared for and of their schools into the education system, and the development of new roles for the expertise of the teachers currently teaching in special schools.

    Secondly work on teacher attitudes, techniques of curriculum analysis and development and classroom management in mainstream schools in order to foster non-segregation of those pupils already attending them and more ready acceptance of positive integration when the time comes.

2. The length of and emphasis on theory in current teacher education courses result in teachers feeling that their expertise focuses on particular pupils and situations. Other pupils and situations require other expertise. This can readily lead to the assumption of an in-child locus of any learning difficulties. Put simply, the curriculum has been centrally determined by experts, the teachers have a lengthy and comprehensive training from well qualified academics in the pedagogy of education and subject didactics, the schools are well equipped with textbooks, so clearly if a child doesn't learn the fault must lie within him or her or with the parents. Poorer achievements by children from socially disadvantaged homes validate this proposition as does the current availability of special pedagogues, logopaedists, neurologists, dentists and the like in most schools.

3. The Lithuanian people have just won their freedom and whilst they recognize that there are problems in their country they are rightly determined that they will find Lithuanian solutions to those problems. Our role is to present them with examples of good practice in inclusive education and the teacher training structures that underlie it.

4. Course and curriculum development in the area of SLD and possibly EBD must be handled very sensitively, building on the considerable skills and commitment of the teachers and carers currently in the schools.

The implications of these developments have been fed back to the appropriate deans of faculty and heads of department at the SPI who will develop new courses in collaboration with colleagues from the MMU and IUFM. The model to be adopted is that of 'continuing professional development'. There will be a shorter initial qualification with a greater emphasis on the teachers' reflecting on the direct results of their own practice and on what such reflection suggests for their future professional development needs. This will involve earlier placement of students in schools on a 'gradualist' basis and more involvement of teachers in those schools in the courses.

Theory will have a much clearer link to practice, and the issues of the role of curriculum content and delivery in the creation of learning difficulties for pupils will be examined. The teachers in their early years of teaching will have continued contact with the SPI and in-service work will be a natural part of their professional development. A recent 'mobility' by senior tutors from the SPI to both the UK and France resulted in open-minded discussion of these issues and a welcome willingness to contemplate quite radical changes. The following are already in effect.

INITIAL TEACHER EDUCATION

- The education of pupils with PMLD has become an integral part of the course on pedagogy. This used to be an optional course but is now part of core studies.
- A course at master's level on 'Integration of Pupils with SEN' was offered within the Faculty of Education for the first time in 1993–4.
- An optional course on 'Education of Pupils with SEN in Mainstream Schools' has been initiated for in-service teacher training students.
- The courses for students training to be pre-school teachers now contain a greater element on cooperative socialization and early integration.
- From 1994 all students entering SPI have had an introductory course on special education. Students training to teach in primary schools have a new course, 'The Basics of Special Pedagogy'.
- A new course on 'Special Education and Logopaedics' has been developed.
- In the courses for logopaedists the terminology and classification of speech and language disorders have been updated to reflect modern thinking and practice. New techniques for use with children who are without speech or who stammer have been introduced.
- Courses to train teachers to work with children and young people with visual impairments have been introduced into the Faculty of Special Education. Courses for teachers of pupils with hearing impairment are actively being developed.
- Changes to general education courses within the Faculty of Education are being introduced to enable beginning teachers to become competent in the education of all abilities of pupils.

Over all the courses there is an increased emphasis on self-organized project work rather than formal theoretical lecturing. There have also been developments in the school-based elements of the courses offered within the Faculties of Education and Special Education. Experience with pupils with MLD, SLD, or PMLD is now offered to all students in the Faculty of Special Education. All students taking initial courses have experience in integrated mainstream classes.

IN-SERVICE TEACHER EDUCATION

*   A new programme for the in-service training of special pedagogues has been introduced at both Republic and Siauliai levels. A shorter course on the organization of support for integrated children has also been introduced.
*   A new Department of Social Pedagogy and Psychology has been founded and is being actively developed in 1994–5.

There have been other spin-offs from the project. A major international postgraduate seminar on the training of teachers of 'British studies' (English) was held at the SPI in June 1994. A symposium of teacher educators from most of the universities in Lithuania was held in Vilnius to consider 'the place of psychology and pedagogy in teacher education'. The Open Lithuania Fund provided the money for three tutors from the MMU to give lead lectures and support discussions. There will be continuing work by three of the groups set up at the symposium. There have been consultations and staff development sessions at the Vilnius and Siauliai Centres of the Republican Diagnostic Service. The main results of this have been the policy decision that all future reports emanating from the service will have a concluding section containing clear curricular implications for the teachers of the pupil assessed. The service is also changing from the Wechsler Intelligence Scale for Children (WISC) to the British Abilities Scale as its major standardized assessment instrument and consequently is translating and restructuring it on a Lithuanian basis. There has also been consideration of the use of Goodman's 'Miscue Analysis' as a method for teachers to use in helping pupils with reading difficulties. This work is to be developed into a consideration of 'specific reading difficulties' (dyslexia) in English and Lithuanian. Most recently there have been discussions with parents' associations for pupils with disabilities about the provision of what in the UK would be called 'respite care'. Here schemes using local community involvement on a volunteer basis were discussed and contacts facilitated with the volunteer organizers of such schemes in the UK.

From France has come the involvement of the CMUDD (Centre Médico-universitaire Daniel Douaday), a major medical centre for the treatment and rehabilitation of spinal injuries. The Centre has relationships with a network of schools for pupils with physical disabilities and close connections with the Grenoble local authority. Whilst the CMUDD itself works at the very frontiers of high technology, its philosophy is that of the reintegration of the individual into the community in the shortest possible time. They have used their skills and understandings to help their Lithuanian colleagues to work with existing or developed resources rather than trying to transfer costly and inappropriate technological solutions, fulfilling again the principle of a 'client-centred' not an 'expert' solution.

The constant theme of all our work in Lithuania is the close interweaving of theory and practice and the respectability of personal theory developed from reflection on coherent articulated practice. We aim to empower the teachers by encouraging them to have confidence in their personal expertise and not to look constantly for the advice of 'experts'. As Marie Černá said during the seminar from which this book is derived, 'The professionalism of the teacher ... is manifested in the skill objectively to evaluate the educational process, analyse the successfulness of his activity, generalise the acquired experience and compare it with educational theory.' If we can develop this professionalism and substitute it for brittle 'expertism' our project will stand a good chance of success.

REFERENCES

Billig, M., Condor, S., Edwards, D., Gane, M., Middleton, D. and Radley, A.(1988) *Ideological Dilemmas*. London: Sage.
Fulcher, G. (1989) *Disabling Policies?* London: Falmer Press.
Johnson, M. (1994) 'Pupils with learning difficulties in schools: needs, rights and democracy'. *Proceedings of the Siauliai International Conference*, January. pp. 62–79.
Johnson, M. (1995) *Psychology and Teacher Education*. Vilnius: Mokykla.
Johnson, M. and Martineniene, R. (1994) *It's Our Class and We Like It: the Use of Fraser's 'My Class Inventory' in a Lithuanian School*. Vilnius: Mokykla.
Mosley, J. (1993) *Turn Your School Around*. Wisbech: Learning Development Association.
Norwich, B. (1993) 'Ideological dilemmas in SEN: practitioners' views'. *Oxford Review of Education*, **19**, 4. pp. 527–46.

Part III

Training for Specific Needs

Chapter 9

Training Needs of Teachers Working with Emotionally Disturbed Children

Monika A. Vernooij

INTRODUCTION

Mainstreaming handicapped children in regular settings is a tendency in international education politics that has been implemented quite successfully not only in Europe. The results, however, show that most emotionally disturbed and severely emotionally disturbed children cannot be taught in regular classes (Peterson *et al.*, 1983; Paul, 1985; Wood, 1989). Their emotional and social maladjustment causes too many problems for themselves as well as for their classmates and their teachers. So it is not surprising that most students with behaviour disorders are being taught in special education placements.

Children with behaviour disorders and emotional disturbances are children who display behaviours that deviate from the normal and generally expected behaviour and who therefore are handicapped in their psychological and social development and their academic performance – despite their usually average to high intelligence. The term 'behavioural disturbance' was created in Paris in 1950 during the First International Congress for Psychiatry. It is a collective term for disturbances that are in part of a medical nature, partly of a mental/emotional (in German *seelisch*) nature, and partly of a social nature, and that are expressed in behaviour.

The education of children with behaviour disorders is still a young science. As illustrated by its short history, it has always been tied very closely to the psychiatric field, with certain areas clearly overlapping. It also has to rely on findings in psychology, especially those of applied psychology (Vernooij, 1984, 1990, 1992, 1993, 1994).

Teachers working with emotionally disturbed children cannot meet the many demands of their job without special training. Besides having to fulfil curricular requirements, i.e. instilling knowledge and developing practical skills, they have to integrate into the classes specific measures that meet the special needs of (severely) emotionally disturbed children. The call for individualized teaching and learning, following the notion of the Individual Education Plan first promoted in the seventies, takes on a special importance with regard to these children and young adults.

THERAPY-ORIENTED SPECIAL EDUCATION (TOS)

During my ten years of teaching in special education schools, I have again and again experienced how closely related special education is to therapeutic intervention. The teaching experience shows that an adequate special education programme for these children and young adults must consist of therapy-oriented special education. By this I mean that any educational action needs to be based on expert knowledge of the subject matter, knowledge of teaching methods and psychological-therapeutic competence. Psychological-therapeutic competence does not mean that the teacher should become a pseudo-therapist in class. It means rather that basic therapeutic concepts and their educational application in special education classes should strongly influence the knowledge of teaching methods.

With the wide variety of basic concepts available, it is hardly possible to commit oneself to a single one. The spectrum reaches from psychology of the unconscious, behaviourist and cognitive concepts to communications and system theories, as well as tendencies in humanistic psychology. It is my intention to present a number of basic therapeutic concepts and their possible educational applications and uses, and to leave the decision as to which particular concept or combination of concepts (for example, depth or cognitive psychology) for the individual teacher to choose.

TOS is a form of teaching that leaves scope for the individual to take action and gain experience. The only requirements are:

- that the classes contain therapeutic elements;
- that the basis for action reflects at least one therapeutic concept and its educational application;
- that education, that is, upbringing and training in academic skills, has priority over therapy. This means that from an anthropological point of view the human being remains first of all a being in need of education and not of therapy.

Regardless of the viewpoint from which we observe deviating behaviour, the general consensus is that the way children are brought up and educated plays an important role in the development of behaviour disorders. Therefore attempts should be made to cure these disorders by means of education and teaching methods. Work in special education is not the repair of broken-down organisms but the correction of a development process gone wrong (see Vernooij, 1987, p. 16). As a result, this work takes on broader educational objectives that are both the result of a general rethinking process and a direct consequence of the specific disorders and difficulties of the child.

If we define education as a planned and systematic process in which the goal is to form an independent, responsible and sociable personality by educational means through the introduction of necessary knowledge and skills, then the re-education process is not started until the development (unfolding) of the personality has already been damaged (see Mücke and Steinbrecher, 1957, p. 21ff.; Vernooij, 1987, p.15). Therapy, however, can generally be seen as a methodical, systematic process during which psychological means are used to influence both the structure of the human psyche and the behaviour patterns of the human being in order to heal these disorders.

The purpose of re-education by special educationalists is not to promote recovery but to correct upbringing. In particular with regard to the pedagogic means applied to children and young adults with deviating behaviour, the line between therapy and special education is often obscure. Among other reasons this derives from the fact that their primary goals are identical. Both re-education and therapy aim at development which relates to the transformation of personality but they use different means and methods (see Vernooij, 1987). In education, the emphasis is on the learning process; in psychotherapy it is on working through experiences and conflicts.

The teaching method based on the TOS principles initiates learning processes which redirect development processes that have gone wrong into different (the right?) channels, that is they correct them, reactivate stagnating developments and continue general developments not affected by disorders. In this context, the role of the teacher is that of an initiator or animator and a supportive and encouraging companion.

TRAINING NEEDS FOR TEACHERS IN CLASSES OF (SEVERELY) EMOTIONALLY DISTURBED CHILDREN

Initiating learning processes is particularly difficult in the special school. Emotionally disturbed, yet usually highly sensitive children relate more strongly to their teacher than do children in regular schools. This means that the reciprocity of conflicts in relationships and discipline assumes more weight. A specific characteristic in the teacher will bring out a specific response in the students, and vice versa. The personality of the teachers, their attitudes, values, feelings, and the way these express themselves in the teachers' behaviour, are all important. Therefore students who choose to teach in special schools need to attend seminars on self-exploration and self-evaluation.

In connection with TOS and the psychological and therapeutic knowledge required for it, the following areas in teacher training take on a special importance:

Personality competence (knowledge of one's own personality)
–   to know one's attitudes, values, prejudices, feelings and expectations, strengths and weaknesses;
–   to be able to think ahead and therefore to be able to control and direct one's actions.
Technical competence (possession of expert knowledge)
–   theory of basic therapeutic concepts;
–   educational preparation of those concepts;
–   ability to handle matters in an educational and therapeutic way.
Analytical competence (ability to analyse situations properly)
–   ability to perceive and analyse situations with regard to their social interconnect-ions and conflicts and to notice possible conflicts and their signals;
–   ability to structure and direct the situation;
–   ability to make adequate decisions and take action.
Pragmatical competence (ability to react appropriately)
–   knowledge and control of behaviour expressed by oneself;
–   availability of a multitude of flexible behaviour patterns for different problem-solving situations.

Personality skills

The development and training of personality skills can be done in three steps: first of all, an insight into one's own personality with all its possibilities and limitations has to be gained through role-play, training in communication skills, and self-exploration seminars. Increased awareness of one's personality in connection with the uncovering of motivational factors is a prerequisite for a competent personality.

The second step is exploring oneself in the role of a teacher, in interactions with the students. Individual characteristics or weaknesses already discovered during general self-exploration should be taken into consideration: for example the difficulty many young people have in setting limits when dealing with others and in staying within those limits.

One day a week is set aside for hands-on training in the special school. The students' teaching activity is recorded on audio and/or on video tape and then evaluated, with the main focus being on the teacher's personality. In the example mentioned above, this would mean that the recorded behaviour is evaluated with regard to setting limits and being consistent.

A third step is to train the students, both in invented situations and in the teaching situation with children, in the ability to anticipate and evaluate situations properly and in keeping their emotions under control when responding to a situation.

Emotionally disturbed children need to have limits set for them: they require emotional stability and a structured environment since they may not be capable of structuring their own environment and their own actions. They are generally deeply insecure children who require clear limits, emotional reliability and a structured environment in order to become more confident.

Technical competence

Technical competence is taught in theoretical seminars. I started a series of lectures in 1987 that stretches over five semesters: 'Basic Therapeutic Concepts and Their Application in (Special) Education I–V'. The subjects covered are as follows:

- psychoanalysis (Freud);
- individual psychology (Adler);
- classic and cognitive behaviour therapy (Skinner, Bandura and Walters, Beck, Lazarus);
- special types of basic therapeutic concept (Ellis, rational-emotive therapy; Rogers, client-centred therapy; Berne, transactional analysis; Frankl, logotherapy);
- systematic approaches/family therapy (Selvini-Palazzoli, Stierlin, Minuchin, Satir, Watzlawik).

Since 1990 classes have lasted three hours each, a two-hour lecture on the theory and one hour of training exercises to practise educational and therapeutical skills. The intense discussion of various basic therapeutic concepts and of their theories of development and views of human nature increases the knowledge of oneself and, as a side effect, initiates and activates personal development. This not only provides the students with the theoretical basis necessary for TOS but also enables them to choose one direction of therapy or a double combination. Efficient educational work with severely emotionally disturbed and emotionally disturbed children can only be done if teachers are able to choose methods and types of teaching that correspond to their personality.

Experience shows that the ability to grasp a situation in its full complexity (and not just parts of it) is rarely trained in young teachers. But especially in classes with emotionally disturbed children, this ability is very important. To approach a situation with circumspection requires a mental stability, a self-awareness and a confidence that a novice simply cannot possess. Another factor essential to a special education teacher's ability to grasp a complex situation is what Thorndike (1926) called 'social intelligence' – the ability to grasp a situation's social structuring and its atmosphere, to evaluate it and to react appropriately. The mental process on which social intelligence is based consists of four major elements:

* a differentiating perception of people and the behaviour they express;
* a realistic awareness of the complex structure of the whole situation, or at least of parts of it, including its outer framework, its atmosphere and one's own position in it;
* evaluation of the situation, with regard to the feelings involved (positive or negative, cheerful or sad, pleasant or unpleasant, threatening or not), to its meaning for the evaluating person and to one's own capacity to take action;
* anticipating evaluation of the social consequences of one's actions.

Teachers can be trained in these mental abilities in several steps:

* working with pictures that show social contexts in which the conflict valency in relationships between two or more people is clearly visible at first, and hidden as training advances;
* working with scenes, either in the form of movie scenes or role-play, with a similar valency;
* working with specific video recordings done in classes with emotionally disturbed children;
* evaluation of one's own teaching performance, above all in order to check one's ability to understand social situations and the conflicts that occur in them.

It is important to find more alternative ways of acting on all levels and actively to play out their consequences in the social context.

Pragmatical competence

This is included in all previous training steps. Self-knowledge is expanded within the framework of personality training. Specific training in the mutual observation of gestures and facial expressions can first be done by the students in group work and later on in supervised classes. This training leads to the control and if necessary modification of the expressed behaviour, and is a necessary addition to personality competence.

Technical competence in certain selected basic therapeutic concepts determines specific behaviours. However, there is never just one correct and binding way of intervening; competence behaviour should be influenced by one's personality or derived from theory, reactions to particular situations and generally known and feasible problem-solving strategies.

The motives for taking action should be brought into harmony. Role-play can be a means of reducing the possible dominance of behaviour patterns based on personality and of practising the directed use of action based on theory.

CATEGORIES FOR THE EDUCATIONAL PREPARATION OF BASIC THERAPEUTIC CONCEPTS

Several categories of preparation have to be applied if basic therapeutic concepts are to be educationally effective and usable.

I have established six such categories:

1. the *anthropological category* of preparation, which aims to identify the view of human nature and of the mental development of the human being latent in various basic theories; for example, human beings as determined by their drives (Freud), or as responsible people (Adler, Berne), or as organisms that can be manipulated (Skinner);
2. the *diagnostic category*, which aims to discover criteria for mental disturbances and mental health, as well as possible instruments for diagnosis, for example projective or standardized procedures;
3. the *selective category*, which aims to find those elements of theory that are of importance to education and could be applied in classes, for example assertiveness training in behaviour therapy or the method of association;
4. the *limitations category*, which aims to identify the limits of therapy; for example, that behaviour therapy addresses behaviour only, or that systematic approaches do not include individual therapy;
5. the *methodological category*, which aims to find out how important theory elements are applied in the teaching situation; for example, how classes are structured, what their contents are, and what methods are used;
6. the *evaluation category*, which aims to find ways of checking and screening therapeutically oriented action in special education with regard to development and changes in the children's personalities.

My experience shows that nearly all basic psychotherapeutic concepts can be prepared in this way for use in (special needs) education.

REFERENCES

Mücke, R. and Steinbrecher, W. (1957) *Das Gemeinschaftsschwierige Kind in Schule und Heim.* Berlin/Neuweid/Darmstadt.

Paul, J.L. (1985) 'Where are we in the education of emotionally disturbed children?' *Behaviour Disorders*, **10**, 145–51.

Peterson, R.L. *et al.* (1983) 'Cascade of services model and emotionally disabled students'. *Exceptional Children*, **49**, 404–8.

Thorndike, E.L. (1926) *The Measurement of Intelligence.* New York.

Vernooij, M.A. (1984) *Schulische Institutionen für Verhaltensgestörte* (Historischer Abriss). Hagen: Fernuniversität-Gesamthochschule.

Vernooij, M.A. (1987) 'Therapie oder sonderpädagogisches Handeln bei Kindern und Jugend-lichen mit Verhaltensstörungen?' *Zeitschrift für Individualpsychologie*, **12**, 14–21.

Vernooij, M.A. (1990) 'Leben als Risikofeld – Kompetenzen zur Orientierung und Gestaltung'. In A. Möckel and A. Müller (eds) *Erziehung zur rechten Zeit*. Würzburg: Bentheim-Verlag.

Vernooij, M.A. (1992) *Hampelliese – Zappelhans: Problemkinder mit Hyperkinetischem Syndrom*. Bern/Stuttgart: Verlag Paul Haupt.

Vernooij, M.A. (1993) 'Verhaltensgestörtenpädagogik – gestern – heute – morgen'. *Die Sonderschule*, **38**, 200–10.

Vernooij M.A. (1994) 'Das Überangepasste Kind oder: Wie eine Käthe-Kruse-Puppe'. In R. Winkel (ed.) *Schwierige Kinder – Problematische Schüler*. Hohengehren: Schneider-Verlag.

Wood, F.H. (1989) 'Learning and teaching: the special teacher of emotionally disturbed and behaviourally disordered students'. In S. Braaten, *et al.* (eds) *Celebrating the Past, Preparing for the Future: 40 Years of Serving Students with Emotional and Behavioural Disorders*. Minneapolis: Minnesota Council for Children with Behavioural Disorders.

Chapter 10

Specific Learning Difficulties: Implications of Research Findings for the Initial and In-service Training of Teachers

Peter D. Pumfrey

CONTEXT

In education, few topics are more controversial than that of specific learning difficulties (hereafter SpLD). The syndrome has been described as 'Unseen, unexpected and unrelenting'. It is considered to be synonymous with specific developmental dyslexia (SDD) by some workers, and voluntary organizations concerned with SpLD (dyslexia) exist in most European countries. The European Dyslexia Association publishes *Euro News Dyslexia*, subtitled '*The Official Journal of the European Dyslexia Association, an International Organization for Specific Learning Disabilities*'. A similar position is adopted in the UK by the British Dyslexia Association and the Dyslexia Institute. Despite this, controversy still surrounds the labels 'specific learning difficulties' and 'specific developmental dyslexia'.

Listen to the words of a parent:

> My child has problems in learning how to read, write and spell. There's no reason that I can see. He's unhappy. He needs help. I don't care what you call this problem – specific learning difficulties, dyslexia, or whatever. We all know it's a real misery-making monster. Please do something to help, and quickly.

(Pumfrey and Reason, 1992)

In this country, the existence of SpLD and SDD is recognized in law. Despite this, legitimate professional disagreements exist concerning its nature, identification and alleviation. The legal acceptance of both conditions gives education authorities responsibilities for identifying and alleviating such disabilities. Teachers have a prime responsibility. It follows that both initial teacher training (ITT) and in-service education for teachers (INSET) must address continuing professional preparation in this field.

In the UK, the policy of integrating pupils with disabilities means that the majority of children with special educational needs are educated in mainstream schools. Literacy is one of the foundations of mainstream education. It is acknowledged as an amplifier of human abilities and a central educational objective for all pupils. Literacy enhances the individual both materially and culturally. To be illiterate in our society is to be marginalized, disempowered and devalued. Literacy enriches: illiteracy impoverishes. Specific learning difficulties and/or specific developmental dyslexia typically demotivate, debilitate and frequently depress the individual. Understandably, parents are deeply concerned (Stoel, 1990).

In England and Wales, a National Curriculum was established by law under the provisions of the Education Reform Act 1988. Each of ten curriculum subjects has its own programme of study (curriculum), attainment targets and statements of attainments (objectives) and a variety of assessment procedures. Within this overall curriculum, English is deemed a core component. Almost all subjects in the curriculum make heavy demands on literacy skills. In principle, the curriculum is also one to which all pupils are entitled (National Curriculum Council, 1989, 1990, 1993).

How accessible is such a curriculum to pupils having SpLD? What can be done to enable their teachers to help such pupils acquire more effective literacy skills?

Under the provisions of the Education Act 1981 and its related regulations and circulars, the state educational system is charged with the identification and alleviation of special educational needs. In theory, this end is achieved primarily through its schools and the LEA specialist support services. The strategy advocated involves differentiation: 'There is a necessity for differentiated tasks appropriate to individual pupils' ability, aptitude and developmental stage. Meeting these needs is the major responsibility of all teachers' (Barthorpe and Visser, 1991 p. 89).

SpLD is recognized as one sub-set of special educational needs, and teachers in initial training are required to take a course concerned with SEN. In general, it is only after some years of experience as a qualified teacher that individuals undertake further specialist courses to develop expertise in the identification and alleviation of SpLD. For legal reasons, the formal validation of such courses is important.

EFFECTIVE TEACHING

The topic of specific learning difficulties is highly controversial. The effective teacher of pupils with specific learning difficulties must be informed concerning the theoretical bases and the research evidence bearing on these controversies. The condition has been defined as a variable syndrome. The existence of any condition requires that empirical evidence meeting at least one of the following four requirements be met. The concept and condition known as SpLD can be said to exist to the extent that there exists a *distinctive*:

- aetiology
- pattern of presenting symptoms
- prognosis
- response to interventions

Disagreements between professionals in relation to these issues lead to variations in the estimated incidence of SpLD. Inevitably, definition determines incidence. Even if professional agreement existed concerning the first three of the above conditions, it does not follow that effective interventions exist. It is the effective interventions that most interest parents, pupils and politicians. The search for interventions should be based on theoretically derived procedures that can be evaluated in the crucibles of the classroom and the clinic.

By itself, being able to help children with SpLD learn to read, write and spell, is not enough. In relation to communication in general and literacy in particular, as a professional the teacher is also required to conceptualize and operationalize, to identify, predict and alleviate problems, and to communicate with other interested parties, including professionals, parents, pupils and politicians. Such professionalism requires the integration of theory and classroom practice. Starting during a teacher's initial training, such integration represents a lifetime's commitment to continuing professional development by the teacher. It includes the following forms of learning:

- an appreciation of the interrelatedness of all aspects of development that apply to all children;
- an awareness of the similarities and differences between the skilled teacher, the child learning to read and pupils with SpLD;
- a knowledge of the patterns of quantitative and qualitative inter- and intra-individual differences characterizing pupils with SpLD;
- an awareness of the demotivational effects of SpLD;
- openness to the contributions of other professionals in the identification and alleviation of SpLD.

RESEARCH: A NATIONAL ENQUIRY INTO SPECIFIC LEARNING DIFFICULTIES

In collaboration with the British Psychological Society, the Centre for Educational Guidance and Special Needs of the University of Manchester has carried out a wide-ranging survey of policies and practices concerning the nature, identification and alleviation of SpLD in England and Wales (Pumfrey and Reason, 1992). The study involved a team of eleven qualified and experienced educational psychologists.

In addition to an historical overview and the identification of current concerns, psychological, psycho-educational and psychomedical approaches to identification and alleviation of SpLD were reviewed. Other data collected included returns from 79 out of 106 local education authorities concerning their policies on SpLD. Replies from 882 educational psychologists concerning their views and practices were also elicited. Further, detailed responses were obtained from the Department of Education and Science (now the Department for Education) and a wide range of professional and voluntary organizations concerning the nature, identification and alleviation of SpLD. Dispensations in relation to public examinations were also studied.

The following section presents selected findings concerning various approaches to the identification and alleviation of SpLD.

RESEARCH: PROMISING AVENUES

Research-based interventions

The DECP (Department for Education Code of Practice) survey included an open-ended question to key professional organizations concerning teaching methods of value in alleviating SpLD. The responses included reference to a wide range of named methods and materials, based on the researchs of particular workers.

Only one approach gained the commendation of all organizations. This was the individualized multisensory approach that originated in the work of Fernald and Keller (1921). This led to an extremely influential book: *Remedial Techniques in the Basic School Subjects* (Fernald, 1943). The resurgence of interest in this work led to it being reprinted in 1971. Instructional systems that systematically integrated visual, auditory, kinaesthetic and tactile sense modalities were developed. The great flexibility of such multisensory approaches is clear. So too is its individualized orientation, whereby the most promising combination of information-processing sense modalities can be utilized.

Established specialist approaches

Well-established teaching programmes for pupils with SpLD include the Orton-Gillingham Method, the Gillingham-Stillman Alphabetic Method, 'Alpha to Omega', the Edith Norrie Letter Case, the Bangor Programme, the Fernald Multisensory Approach, Bannantyne's Colour Phonetics, the Hickey Method, the Peabody Rebus Reading Programme and Neville-Brown's Icon Approach. Descriptions of these are available (Pumfrey, 1991). The list represents only a fraction of approaches currently being practised (Pumfrey and Elliott, 1993; Pumfrey and Reason, 1992). Advanced training for teachers in a number of these techniques is currently receiving impetus in the UK because of the effects of recent legislation and increased parental concern.

Aptitude and Instruction Interactions (AIIs)

Finding which methods best suit which pupils at particular stages in their journeys to literacy is a major professional responsibility faced by all teachers of all pupils. Put formally, it is the ongoing search for Aptitude and Instruction Interactions (AIIs). In the interests of efficiency, AIIs relevant to particular groups are of theoretical and practical importance.

Children with SpLD have many learning characteristics in common with all children (Bradley, 1990; Bryant, 1990; Goswami, 1993). They also differ from their peers in the ways in which they learn (Tyler, 1990). The focus of research into sub-types of SpLD is on aspects of 'within child' information processing. There is considerable evidence that pupils with SpLD are not a homogeneous group. The identification of sub-types of SpLD is highly relevant to the efficient provision of effective interventions. Diagnostic approaches that claim to identify distinctive categories of pupils with SpLD have been developed (e.g. Boder and Jarrico, 1982; Elliott, 1989; Bakker, 1990). The validity and utility of two of these are currently being studied with schoolchildren in the Manchester area identified as having learning difficulties. Different teaching programmes are being developed for use with groups of pupils who have different types of learning difficulties.

Recently, three sub-groups of children with SpLD have been identified on the basis of their test results on the British Ability Scales (Tyler, 1990). The largest grouping was that referred to as having a 'sequential processing deficit'. The second distinctive grouping was characterized by what was called 'holistic retrieval of information'. The third group manifests deficits in mixed visual-spatial and linguistic processing.

When a profile of abilities is identified, deciding the balance between working on relative strengths, weaknesses or some combination of both remains a challenge to which there is no consensus response.

Research: hemisphere-specific stimulation and hemisphere-alluding stimulation

Bakker (1990) theorizes that learning to read is a bi-hemispheric adventure. The early stages are associated more with right-hemisphere electrophysiological activity. Left-hemisphere activity develops during later stages. Right hemisphere activity is predominantly perceptual; left hemisphere functions are more associated with semantic and syntactic functions. Initial reading requires close attention to the perceptual features of text. In learning to read, hemispheric mediation begins with the right-hemisphere activities being dominant. When perceptual analysis of text has become automated, the left hemispheric functions play a key role. Thus perceptual factors are predictive of initial reading whereas more advanced levels involve linguistic functions. These ideas fit, in part, with a three-stage model of reading and spelling development (Frith and Snowling, 1983).

Bakker argues that some children fail to progress in reading because they do not make the necessary shift in hemispheric functioning. They continue to depend on perceptually dominated right-hemispheric strategies. He calls these children 'P-type' dyslexic. Other children learning to read may, from the start, use left-hemispheric strategies. These he calls 'L-type' dyslexics. They read in a hurry and produce many substantive errors such as omissions, additions and substitutions. Bakker claims that approximately 60 to 70 per cent of dyslexic children can be classified as either P or L type.

The above ideas have led towards methods of treating these two forms of dyslexia. Hemispheric alluding stimulation (HAS) uses adapted classroom reading materials. Texts are made perceptually demanding for L-type dyslexics by, for example, mixing lower- and upper- case letters within words. For P-type dyslexics, texts are made phonetically, semantically or syntactically demanding. The first results of using HAS with single case studies are promising (Kappers and Bos, 1990).

At Manchester, a small-scale study into the effects of hemisphere alluding stimulation on eight P-type dyslexic pupils has recently been completed (Filippatou, 1992). The experimental design involved four matched pairs of pupils in experimental and control groups tested before and after a period of intervention. The analyses showed significant interactions between occasions and groups in respect of the words read under rapid and untimed presentations of single words, and of the number of words spelled correctly. The intervention appeared to be effective for only two of the four pupils. The findings underline the point that extensive replication is essential before any definite conclusions can be drawn concerning the efficacy of HAS on P-type dyslexic pupils. Such a field study is now being carried out by a doctoral student in the School of Education at the University of Manchester.

An unresolved debate concerning the balance between concentrating on a pupil's cognitive 'strengths' or 'weaknesses' in alleviating SpLD is highlighted by this work, and larger-scale work involving three local education authority learning support services is in progress.

Coloured overlays and tinted lenses (glasses)

The clinical evidence that a number of individual pupils have been significantly helped by the use of coloured overlays and lenses cannot easily be overlooked. Such reports have come from a range of informed and competent research workers specializing in colour perception and from highly experienced teachers in various countries.

Further and more rigorous follow-up studies of individual pupils who have used coloured overlays and/or tinted lenses are needed. Their management in educational establishments presents considerable problems for the individual pupil. Teachers who have knowledge of the progress of pupils in their schools who have been assessed and who have been recommended to use overlays and/or tinted lenses could provide valuable feedback to colleagues. This could be done either through the correspondence columns of professional journals or direct to the author of the present chapter (Pumfrey, 1993a).

In this complex and legitimately controversial field, theory, research and practice will continue to develop. In the meantime, if coloured overlays or tinted lenses have positive effects in alleviating reading difficulties with particular individuals, their use should not be eschewed because the reasons for such effects are at present ill-understood.

IMPLICATIONS FOR INITIAL TEACHER TRAINING AND IN-SERVICE TRAINING

SpLD is not a single condition. There can be no educational panacea. Each child with SpLD has a unique pattern of cognitive strengths and weaknesses. If such learning difficulties are recognized by teachers, progress without tears is possible. Progress without great effort and commitment is highly improbable. As many pupils who manifest SpLD know, they can become literate, but it requires the support of the child's family and teachers (Pumfrey, 1993b). The use of word processors and computer-assisted learning holds considerable promise (Innes, 1990). There are, however, no guarantees of success (Hampshire, 1990).

The many implications for teacher education of research into SpLD lead to the following six objectives:

- raising teachers' awareness of the nature of SpLD and of the distress it can cause;
- enhancing teachers' knowledge of the nature and extent of both inter- and intra-individual differences of pupils using a range of diagnostic assessment techniques;
- increasing teachers' understanding of the options for intervention available and their sensitivity to the importance of identifying Aptitude and Instruction Inter-actions;

- developing competence in promising pedagogies through advanced courses for qualified teachers;
- accepting that other groups of professionals can contribute towards understanding the nature of SpLD and minimizing its adverse effects;
- accepting that, imperfect as our understanding of SpLD is, teachers can do much to help individual pupils recognize the condition, minimize its adverse effects, and learn to live with it.

For the teaching profession, these objectives represent a long-term strategy. The distinction between professional responsibilities characterized during initial teacher training and the subsequent continuing professional development expected by, and of, qualified teachers, is more a matter of emphasis than of kind. The development of a National Curriculum to which *all* pupils are entitled, and within which English is a core subject, means that increasing attention has been paid in initial and in-service teacher training to the programmes of study to be followed and the monitoring of standards and progress of individuals and groups (Department of Education and Science and the Welsh Office, 1989).

Should the education of pupils with SpLD be the responsibility of specialist teachers alone? Few would deny that educational expertise is important. The teaching profession comprises many specialisms, which become increasingly differentiated as teachers' interests, knowledge and expertise develop and career opportunities open up. Despite these differences, the profession's communality of concerns in both providing and improving the education of the individual pupil remain two central and shared objectives throughout all professional careers (Hegarty, 1993).

It is this continuing communality of concerns that gives salience to the 'whole-school' approach to addressing special educational needs in general and specific learning difficulties in particular (National Curriculum Council, 1989). In 1994 in the UK, a *Code of Practice on the Identification and Assessment of Special Educational Needs* was published (Department for Education and the Welsh Office, 1994), and in the same year, a complementary circular on *The Organization of Special Educational Provision* (Department for Education, 1994). These consultative documents hold considerable promise for improving the development of policies and practices within all state schools.

Their success will, in large measure, depend on the commitment of schools and teachers. An explicit collective responsibility is required, both in principle and in practice, for the education of all pupils. Coupled with this is the need to develop the professional knowledge and skills required to differentiate delivery of the curriculum to pupils with various and changing special educational needs (Barthorpe and Visser, 1991). The implications for those concerned with both initial teacher training and continuing professional development are considerable. Addressing them will be an ongoing challenge to teacher trainers, and to teachers at all stages of their careers.

At the school level, governors must ensure that the school has a published policy on special educational needs, and its effects must be monitored. Parental involvement and that of voluntary associations concerned with the identification and alleviation of specific learning difficulties (for example dyslexia) are required. A strict timetable for decision-making and evaluation is prescribed. Each school is required to appoint a special educational needs coordinator (SENCO) with important responsibilities for developing policy and provision for pupils with SEN.

Initial and in-service training in special education in general, and in SpLD in particular, are of the essence because the recommended five-stage model for action makes each school, and *all* the staff therein, responsible for stages 1 to 3. These stages do not involve formal assessment, but provide opportunities to establish whether the individual's difficulty can be satisfactorily addressed within the school's own resources and expertise.

At stage 1, class or subject teachers identify or register the possibility of a pupil having a SEN, consult the school's SENCO and take initial action (Townsend, 1994). At stage 2 the SENCO takes leading responsibility for gathering information, coordinating the pupil's programme and working with the pupil's teachers. At stage 3, specialists from outside the school can be brought in to provide additional support. At stages 4 and 5 the local education authority and the school share responsibility in considering whether a multidisciplinary assessment and a statement are required.

The precise definition, and therefore incidence, of SpLD remains controversial (Pumfrey and Reason, 1992). Despite this reservation SpLD represents the largest category of officially recognized disability both in the United Kingdom and elsewhere (including the USA, Australia, Canada and New Zealand). This point underlines the importance of continuing research in the classroom, clinic and laboratory if our ability to conceptualize, identify and alleviate SpLD is to be advanced. Research is central: it is not an optional 'add-on'.

It is worth remembering the pioneer work on integrating research with initial and in-service teacher training initiated some 50 years ago by Professors Schonell, Wall, Kelmer Pringle and their successors at the University of Birmingham School of Education Child Study Centre. That initiative contributed to the formation of the National Association of Remedial Education (NARE). NARE's focus was on the identification and alleviation of underachievement in the basic subjects in general and in literacy in particular (Sampson, 1975). The subsequent amalgamation in the late 1980s of NARE and the Association for Special Education (ASE) to form the National Association for Special Educational Needs (NASEN) has resulted in a large organization that has many members professionally involved in identifying and alleviating SpLD through their membership of local education authority Learning Support Services and School Psychological Services. NASEN's professional journal *Support for Learning* is a valuable source of research-based ideas in this field for both initial and in-service training.

The complementary development of expertise on SpLD (dyslexia) in Britain in the voluntary sector from 1896 to 1993 has recently been summarized (Brooks, 1993). The establishment of the Dyslexia Institute Guild in 1993 provided another important national focus for teachers and other professionals involved in work with pupils with SpLD. It already has a membership of over 600 (Mohammed, 1994). A Council for the Registration of Schools Teaching Dyslexic Pupils has also been established (Crisfield and Smythe, 1994). Collaboration between the City Technology Trust and the Dyslexia Institute has demonstrated the ways in which the benefits of technological innovation can be developed and disseminated to other schools and colleges (Flecker, 1994; Day, 1994).

Advanced courses of training are in increasing demand. It is essential that these have a strong research base. The universities run a considerable variety of such courses, undertake a wide spectrum of research and publish extensively. A number of local education authorities run their own training courses or ones validated by the Royal Society of Arts (RSA) or a university. The RSA Diploma is taught at the Hornsby, Arkell and Watford Centres and elsewhere. In collaboration with Kingston University, the Dyslexia Institute is delivering a postgraduate diploma in various places. The Scottish Dyslexia Trust and the Scottish Office Education Department have provided support to the Moray House Institute of Education for the Centre for Specific Learning Difficulties to develop open learning course materials for postgraduate awards in SpLD offered by Moray House/Heriot Watt University (Reid, 1993, 1994).

With reference to the development of national, local and school policies in the 1990s in England and Wales that are focused on the identification and alleviation of SpLD, important lessons can be learned from the Education Act 1993 (Brooks, 1994). Policies and practices must also be evaluated through research into their efficacy (for example Rack and Walker, 1994). Teachers must know sufficient about research techniques to make informed judgements concerning the validity of what researchers do and report. Perhaps even more important is that teachers need to be informed and confident enough to undertake systematic studies of pupils with SpLD within their own schools.

From the above, it follows that research into both the varied manifestations of SpLD and the efficacy of a school's policy and practices in relation to pupils with SpLD are essential if the criteria of accountability and continuing professional development are to be met by teachers. These complementary interests can be integrated in both initial and in-service teacher training.

Teachers as professionals have responsibilities for special needs education at both the initial and the in-service stages in many European countries. A comment valid for all pupils can unify our thinking. 'If the child cannot learn the way we teach, can we teach the way the child learns?'

My concern has been with SpLD. Despite the uncertainties concerning the nature, identification and alleviation of SpLD, the letter written to the DECP Enquiry by a 10-year-old boy called Zachary (shown opposite), makes an eloquent clinical case for such children (Pumfrey and Reason, 1992).

March 8th

Dear Mr Pumfrey.

I am ten. I did not injoy life until I got hellp because the techer say (thinking thay no evrything) you are lase and norty,,.

Now I am haveing hellp I can rit letters and storys and eveyfing I wont to. But speling is stil a lital bit difacelt.

I fink evre scool shood have a speshal techer that thchis chririn to try and get rid of ther Broblem. When the techer told me to rit I wood sit doon and untik it got difelcelt and sumthing alluay cort my alenchon and I wood mes a round and get told off ond I did not lisk life then.

I have riton a book and I have folocopeed it for you. I am going to rit anuther book and it is about two mice that go to the city and met ampeooth Love

From
Sachary

REFERENCES

Bakker, D.J. (1990) *Neuropsychological Treatments of Dyslexia*. Oxford: Oxford University Press.
Barthorpe, T. and Visser, J. (1991) *Differentiation: Your Responsibility*. Stafford: National Association for Remedial Education Publications.
Boder, E. and Jarrico, S. (1982) *Boder Test of Reading–Spelling Patterns*. New York, Grune & Stratton.
Bradley, L. (1990) 'Rhyming connections in learning to read and spell.' In P.D. Pumfrey and C.D. Elliott (eds) *Children's Difficulties in Reading, Spelling and Writing*. London: Falmer Press.
Brooks, E. (1993) 'The development of expertise on dyslexia in Britain.' In J. Crisfield and I. Smythe (eds) *The Dyslexia Handbook*. Reading: British Dyslexia Association.
Brooks, E. (1994) 'Changes in education, 1994'. *Dyslexia Review*, Autumn, 25–7.
Bryant, P. (1990) 'Phonological development and reading.' In P. D. Pumfrey and C.D. Elliott (eds) *Children's Difficulties in Reading, Spelling and Writing*. London: Falmer Press.
Crisfield, J. and Smythe, I. (1994) *The Dyslexia Handbook, 1993/4*. Reading: British Dyslexia Association.
Day, J. (1994) *A Software Guide for Specific Learning Difficulties*. Coventry: National Council for Education Technology.
Department of Education and Science and the Welsh Office (1989) *National Curriculum: From Policy to Practice*. London: HMSO.
Department for Education (1994) *The Organisation of Special Education Provision* (Circular 6/94). London: DfE.
Department for Education and the Welsh Office (1994) *Education Act 1993. Code of Practice on the Identification and Assessment of Special Educational Needs*. London: DfE
Elliott, C.D. (1989) 'Cognitive profiles of learning disabled children.' *British Journal of Developmental Psychology*, 7, 171–8.
Fernald, G. (1943) *Remedial Techniques in the Basic School Subjects*. New York: McGraw-Hill.
Fernald, G. and Keller, H. (1921) 'Effects of kinaesthetic factors in the development of word recognition'. *Journal of Educational Research*, 4, 335.
Filippatou, D. (1992) 'The effects of hemisphere alluding stimulation (HAS) on P-dyslexic pupils.' Unpublished MEd dissertation. School of Education, University of Manchester.
Flecker, M. (1994) *Doing well with Dyslexia. A Shared Exercise with the Dyslexia Institute and the City Technology Colleges Trust* (Preface by the Secretary of State for Education). London: City Technology Colleges Trust.
Frith, U. and Snowling, M. (1983) 'Reading for meaning and reading for sound in autistic and dyslexic children.' *British Journal of Developmental Psychology*, 1, 329–42.
Goswami, U. (1993) 'Orthographic analogies and reading development'. *The Psychologist*, 6(7), 312–16.
Hampshire, S. (1990) *Every Letter Counts*. Aylesbury: Bantam.
Hegarty, S. (1993) *Meeting Special Needs in Ordinary Schools*, 2nd edn. London: Cassell.
Innes, P. (1990) *Defeating Dyslexia: a Boy's Story*. London: Kyle Cathie.
Kappers, E.J. and Bos, W. (1990) 'Hemisphere-alluding stimulation in two children with dyslexia'. Paper read at the 13th World Congress of Readers, Stockholm, 3–6 July.
Mohammed, M. (1994) 'The Dyslexia Institute Guild'. *Dyslexia Review*, Autumn, 30.
National Curriculum Council (1989) *A Curriculum for All: Curriculum Guidance No. 2*. York: NCC.
National Curriculum Council (1990) *The Whole Curriculum: Curriculum Guidance No. 3*. York: NCC.
National Curriculum Council (1993) *Special Needs and the National Curriculum: Opportunity and Challenge*. York: NCC.
Pumfrey, P.D. (1991) *Improving Children's Reading in the Junior School*. London: Cassell.
Pumfrey, P.D. (1993a) 'Focus on dyslexia: coloured overlays and tinted lenses (glasses)'. *Special*, July. pp. 44–6.

Pumfrey, P.D. (1993b) 'Specific learning difficulties'. In *Working Together at all Ages and Stages*. Rotherham: Rotherham LEA.

Pumfrey, P.D. and Elliott, C.D. (eds) (1993) *Children's Difficulties in Reading, Spelling and Writing*. London: Falmer Press.

Pumfrey, P.D. and Reason, R. (1992) *Specific Learning Difficulties (Dyslexia): Challenges and Responses*. London: Routledge (originally NFER-Nelson, 1991).

Rack, J. and Walker, J. (1994) 'Does Dyslexia Institute teaching work?' *Dyslexia Review*, Autumn, 12–16.

Reid, G. (ed.) (1993) *Specific Learning Difficulties (Dyslexia). Perspectives on Practice*. Edinburgh: Moray House.

Reid, G. (1994) *Specific Learning Difficulties (Dyslexia). A Handbook for Study and Practice*. Edinburgh: Moray House.

Sampson, O.C. (1975) *Remedial Education*. London: Routledge & Kegan Paul.

Stoel, S. van der (ed.) (1990) *Parents on Dyslexia*. Clevedon: Multilingual Matters.

Townsend, J. (1994) *Understanding Dyslexia: a Teacher's Perspective*. London: The Dyslexia Institute.

Tyler, S. (1990) 'Subtypes of specific learning difficulties'. In P.D. Pumfrey and C.D. Elliott (eds) *Children's Difficulties in Reading, Spelling and Writing*. London: Falmer Press.

Chapter 11

Mathematical Learning: a Neglected Theme in Special Education

Olof Magne

CHRIS, ERIK AND THE CASE OF BOB

This chapter will deal with Chris and Erik and their observation of a handicapped student and, later on, their discussion with the group they belonged to during their teacher training. The chapter also examines the intricate web of cognitive processes underlying the training (or educating) of mathematics teachers who intend to tutor disabled students as effectively as possible.

During 1993, a group of future secondary school teachers revolted slightly against certain routines. Their idea was to prepare a study programme with great freedom for the students to compose individual study themes within broader general curricular objectives. I became involved because I was asked to act as an extra tutor to Chris and Erik, who concentrated on mathematics teaching. Both had respectable academic qualifications: Chris had graduated with a dissertation in mathematics and Erik was a civil engineer. Their aim was to be mathematics teachers.

It then happened that both were allotted to a practice period in a class of 16-year-old students, in what in Sweden is called a *gymnasium*, roughly corresponding to the British sixth form or the United States college.

In this class, one student aroused the sympathy and interest of the two young mathematicians. Bob had to use a wheelchair due to cerebral palsy; he could not move his legs. Apparently, he was quite bright. His linguistic ability was good, and he was well informed in history, literature, philosophy and social science. However, in mathematics, Bob functioned very poorly.

Bob's mathematics learning problems were discussed with the mathematics teacher. Chris and Erik devised a scheme to diagnose Bob's mathematical performance and suggested an adequate programme for him. The outcome was a solid study of Bob's mathematical knowledge, interests and motivation. A remarkable thing was that Bob liked to learn mathematics but on a level corresponding with his knowledge. It proved impossible, though, to suggest other than conventional recommendations concerning study methods and learning aids for him.

Later we came up with the idea – or rather principle – that for Bob, *mathematics should be what he needed for his future life*. Bob was firm about his coming career, namely to work in social services, preferably among disabled persons. For Bob, mathematics should mean application to social services. Chris and Erik tried to sell this idea to Bob's mathematics teacher who, however, only reluctantly let himself be persuaded into presenting Bob with social service problems. The teacher said that he had no instructional aids for this purpose, which was true. This was looked upon as failure. Thus, to Chris and Erik, mathematics for disabled students appeared to be a very neglected field of study, at least in Sweden.

During the following check-up by Chris and Erik and their fellow students, they all suggested that research is more or less lacking. If this were put to the test elsewhere it might be found to be true of the education systems in other countries too. When we discussed the needs of the disabled student, we agreed that mathematical learning, as well as teacher education, needed to be changed for the better.

STUDENT TEACHERS DISCUSS

Now, let us look at the mathematical education of a prospective special teacher from the horizon of the student teachers themselves. What would a student teacher think when he or she meets with the problem of how to stimulate and tutor a disabled student to come up to optimal mathematical development?

At the Malmö School of Education my colleagues and I have conducted interviews and experiments with student teachers on their task as teachers of mathematics for disabled pupils. Some suggestions have emerged. This enables us to derive some conclusions as to how special educators should acquire their instructional skills.

Let us now go back to problem-conscious student teachers like Chris and Erik. They will probably ask for answers to key questions that begin with words such as 'why?', 'who?', 'what?' and 'how?' Here therefore are some questions:

Why should special teachers argue that a disabled person needs mathematics?
Who can have the use of such mathematics?
What should special teachers include in the mathematics of individual students?
How should special teachers acquire the necessary knowledge themselves?

Question 1: Why should special teachers argue that a disabled person needs mathematics?

Mathematics – is it needed for children with special educational needs? Or to talk like ordinary people, will 'number work' come in useful for 'children poor at maths'?

So the student teachers discuss the matter. First they look up what is said about mathematics in the school curriculum. They will find two basic aims:

1. To give the pupil a foundation for higher formal mathematical studies at universities, colleges, etc.;

2.   To furnish the pupil with general information about notions of quantity and space for activities of occupation, communication and leisure in common everyday life.

But how will this be put into practice in special education?

The group of student teachers who took part in this discussion were inclined to think that a majority of special teachers may look at mathematical learning as the Cinderella of special education. A common belief seems to be that there are other fields which are more important to practise and learn.

There is no lack of publications on mathematical education for sight-or hearing-impaired, physically, mentally disabled or emotionally disturbed children. But most writers confine themselves to a very limited range of topics, usually to the three themes of calculation with natural numbers, aphasic phenomena and mathematics anxiety. Typically, international conferences seldom contain more than one or two papers on the mathematical behaviour of disabled persons among, say, a thousand presentations.

Paolo Freire (1985), Stieg Mellin-Olsen (1987) and other have maintained that literacy and mathematical competence are valuable and essential for the quality of life of the individual. If mathematical knowledge capital can be enlarged, there is also an increase in the power of the individual to be master of his life. Paolo Freire was an inspired pioneer of educational programmes created in order to raise the oppressed and strengthen international consciousness, offering disabled and deprived persons opportunities to achieve social maturity and an independent life in society. He claimed that mathematics was very much needed.

On the one hand, education can preserve established injustices and barriers and contribute to producing rigid, timid and alienated subordinates. One social group that has little power over the lives of its members is labelled 'mentally handicapped'. Social incompetence and lack of linguistic and numerical communication lead to cultural isolation and deprivation. On the other hand, education may, through socialization and by setting a good example, also build up active consciousness and self-confidence for isolated and deprived human beings. For persons with such labels, it is important that their learning goes beyond mechanical drills or training, as ends in themselves, and that it does not result in shallow consumer routines.

Basically, everything depends on what is the meaning of mathematics. Has society fixed why and what the student must learn? Or is it you and I who have the power to say what mathematics is, based on our needs, interests and ability to think? Bob and many other students may want to learn mathematics in its application to social services. This may be called *social mathematics*. It can be a purposeful answer for many deprived students.

A three-part answer to the 'why?' question could therefore be that:

–   mathematical knowledge is a component of human survival;
–   all students, including students with special educational needs, should learn mathematics according to their individual needs, interest and power of thinking;
–   future mathematical programmes should harmonize with the specific background of the individual, making allowance for social aspects of the subject matter and the social competence of the student.

Question 2: Who can have the use of mathematics according to the discussion on question 1?

Prospective teachers must learn about how children with special educational needs learn. They should go through a learning process about their pupils' learning, as well as acquiring teaching experience.

Researchers seem to agree that there are considerable individual variations in mathematical behaviour among those who are said to have special educational needs. The special teacher must have a good knowledge of these facts. Comparisons between high achievers and low achievers in mathematics display many similar error patterns, for instance:

- All pupils do both correct and incorrect mathematics as a result of thought processes.
- It seems obvious that many inadequate reactions are caused by oversight in all pupils, or an accidental lack of concentration.
- All pupils are working with an apparent striving after meaning (Bartlett's term).
- It is evident that low achievers and underachievers, as well as other pupils, form structures individually and do their problem-solving or computation in accordance with 'schemes' or strategies derived from earlier experiments.
- Divergent shortcomings can be looked upon as individual logical reasoning in the interplay of mathematical contents and pupils' personality.

No less important is the finding that, in some respects, error patterns are dissimilar for high achievers and low achievers. The following three observations seem to be particularly valid:

- Most shortcomings of low achievers are the result of lacking or insufficient logic. Most miscalculations of high achievers are due to oversight.
- Low achievers not only make systematic divergences but, if not given remedial intensive intervention, continue with the same type of behaviour for long periods of time. High achievers seldom diverge systematically and easily abandon error patterns.
- Remediation is a comparatively easy process for high achievers, whereas it is an extremely time-consuming and laborious affair for low achievers.

Special teachers may look upon themselves as detectives in the Wimsey or Poirot tradition in order to deduce from seemingly meaningless or insignificant clues what is going on in the child's mind. As they become better at this observation and detection technique, their effectiveness as teachers will improve. With the help of persistent, devoted diagnosis founded in modern educational philosophy, the special teacher is able to prescribe a valid programme.

Learning is something that takes place in a conscious mind due to active volition. Conceptual discoveries and creative actions are part of mathematical thinking in all human beings. This applies not only to the mathematical thinker but also to the disabled child. In many cases, however, the handicapped child does not reach the higher levels of conceptual knowledge (e.g. Piaget's concrete and formal operations).

We may hypothesize that children with typical disabilities display typical aberrations, but little is known for certain. Blind children are at a disadvantage because they have a visualization handicap and therefore may be inhibited in their efforts to imagine numbers and geometric conceptions. Deaf children may be linguistically impaired; this often leads to a restricted vocabulary and, secondarily, to limited reasoning power. Emotionally disturbed pupils may display a disordered state of mind, and their logical reasoning could become confused; consequently, they may have difficulty in establishing mathematical structures in problem-solving. Motor impairment often inhibits the growth of form perception and geometric notions.

As for mentally disabled children, there is a good deal of information showing that these students have other mathematical strategies than average students (see for instance Janke, 1980). Indeed, they are able to acquire some knowledge in all the main mathematical areas (Magne and Thörn, 1987). Individual differences are considerable.

Most mentally disabled persons have great difficulty in grasping the structure of the decimal system. Their mastery of mathematical expressions is usually extremely low (problem-solving), owing to their reasoning disability. This leads to inadequate strategies in problem-solving. Experiences and conception of numbers are often limited to two-digit natural numbers and very simple relational numbers. Simple visualization and geometry skills can be attained although more complex achievements may be unattainable. Of the four rules, addition is better mastered than other arithmetical operations. Least skill is found in division. Even the simplest cases of probability and algebra are usually not mastered. Desk calculators or computers should always be used instead of pencil and paper computation.

Let us take the case of Anneli. She is what is often called a mentally handicapped child, aged 12. Her teacher has used a lot of sensible ideas and equipment to get her to learn addition tables, but without success. The fault is not her teacher's. She has done her best to foster a sense of thinking, but Anneli has a thinking handicap. She can look and talk very well, but she has shortcomings in her perceptive brain cells and a strange confusion in organizing her recollections or experiences. Similar educational shortcomings may be found in other children with or without special educational needs, for instance sight- or hearing-impaired, motor- or neurologically and emotionally disordered children.

What can Anneli do? It seems first of all necessary to quit the formal way to learn mathematics. The next thing would be to reconsider the type of mathematical learning which she has used. For Anneli and many of her equals, an alternative would be to change the approach to learning fundamentally and concentrate on the social aspects of mathematics.

Question 3: What should special teachers include in the mathematics of individual students?

In the subsequent discussion the 'what?' question was looked upon as a central issue by the student teachers. In these talks the key words turned out to be *social competence*. Let us consider this for mentally retarded children.

Social competence is a name for the degree of independence in a person's daily life. Over and above primary activity for daily living training, social competence means possessing practical attainments of a socially adaptive character. This includes the ability to form and command 'concept systems'. As has been said earlier, an important objective is that by the use of mathematical knowledge the student will reach optimal social emancipation (also Kylén, 1974; Nyborg, 1986).

Nyborg speaks about fundamental concept systems. He argues that concepts may be both verbal and non-verbal and defines a concept as a form of knowledge or knowing which is retained and stored in the mind of the individual and is used by the mind to 'grasp' or understand. The concept system is a set of concepts which is organized into differentiated totalities, composed of principal, subordinate and collateral concepts which are usually organized with the help of symbol combinations. The concept, in Nyborg's sense, may be interpreted psychologically rather than logically. Nyborg has thoroughly explored the learning procedures and conditions of learning in mentally handicapped persons and also described how concept systems begin, are created and consolidated or decomposed in socialization processes.

With regard to the social aspect of mathematical learning, it is fruitful to exemplify fundamental concept systems (according to Nyborg's terminology). Obviously, it is a case of open systems, formed under the influence of their social usefulness: form (round, square), position (horizontal, vertical, seated, erect), quantity (large, small, four; increase, reduce amount), size (height, width, etc.), placement (space, distance, location), co-ordinates, direction, temperature, mass, weight, etc., time, value (including money), speed (velocity, rate, etc.).

Bob and Anneli seemed to be examples of social competence on quite different cognitive levels. Bob would have a programme aiming at professional knowledge within his social interests. His problem is that no available textbook suited him. He should himself take a hand in planning. In theory it might be possible to construct a study course for Bob centred around welfare services, labour market conditions, administrative work and so on, although in practice it is difficult to do this effectively. Exercises should concentrate on analysing practical problems, instead of formal mathematical subject matter. Among mathematical topics, elementary statistics and probability could be used, preferably population studies, as well as the use of formulas in algebra. A low-cost calculator should be the usual instrument for computation. Computers are necessary, particularly in some practical problem-solving. Rote learning of mental pencil and paper type, as algorithmic drill, should be totally avoided. This could be summarized with the catchwords: individualized do-and-think learning, rather than step-by-step procedural learning.

For Anneli mathematics literally means survival learning to achieve independence in her future life. What is needed for Anneli? Perhaps a less formal and a more social and practical approach to learning mathematics. Social competence includes: helping oneself, for example being capable of moving, being successful with hygiene and health; taking care of clothing; providing meals for oneself; transporting oneself; occupying oneself or having a job; communicating with others by language; taking responsibility for oneself and others; collaborating in social activities.

Magne and Thörn (1987) delineate six main behaviour areas associated with mathematics learning:

P-area:	Linguistic representation and problem-solving;
N-area:	Numeration and notation conceptions;
G-area:	Form perception and space representation, body awareness, money, geometry, measuring and units;

ASMD-area:	The four operations;
F-area:	Functions, algebra, equations;
B-area:	Descriptive statistics, probability.

Important social activities can be found in areas P, N, G and ASMD. It would also be useful for every handicapped student to have experience of probability – in gambling, at pools or in a lottery (area B).

Preparing a meal often contains mathematical components (P, N, G and ASMD areas); these areas are also brought into play as *transportation* develops beyond the mere capacity for motor movement. *Linguistic contacts* lead to quantity terms and verbal puzzles, later on to more sophisticated operations involving several mathematical areas (P, G, ASMD); these as well as N occur in *occupation*, which is simple only during the earliest years. *Taking responsibility for oneself* is an area full of complex activities requiring mathematical operations in the P, N and G areas; these together with the B area cover the mathematical tasks of various kinds involved in *collaboration in social activities*.

Many of these individual activities or group duties can be anticipated in school. Anneli can be offered an optional learning programme in cooperation with other school subjects where the development of her social competence should be emphasized. A practical example from disability didactics is the project which Donovan carried out with Australian teenagers in a special school for intellectually disabled pupils (Donovan, 1989, 1990).

There is a risk that the teacher will produce barriers that hinder the students from becoming independent. On the other hand, the educator has the privilege of reducing insecurity and raising the students' feeling that they can seize power over their quality of life. The mathematics teacher should always ask: 'How can mathematics learning be directed at better understanding and transforming reality towards a more human existence for disabled persons?'

Question 4: How should special teachers acquire the necessary knowledge themselves?

What does the education of special teachers look like, as it is represented by the studies of Chris, Erik and their fellow students?

The esteem and time to be afforded to mathematics, as well as the form it should take, are controversial issues among teacher trainers, mainly due to the low priority given to the subject. In Swedish special teacher education, for example, mathematics and its didactics have, at most, 3 per cent of the total teaching time. However, if the social value of mathematics is primarily meant to be important for survival and betterment of the individual being, mathematics learning must be given higher priority.

Mathematical programmes in special teacher education are aimed at one and only one goal: to prepare special teachers to teach mathematics well and efficiently. At first, teachers will have to learn about how handicapped students learn. They must also discuss the philosophy of teaching, acquire indirect teaching experience, learn some psychology and, finally, try out correct systematic interventions on learning in school so that learning can actually take place.

Teacher trainers must also have knowledge of the same kind, at an advanced level certainly. The trainers must go through a learning process about learning, as well as teaching mathematics, showing the student teachers good and efficient ways of learning for pupils with special educational needs.

In their teacher training, Chris and Erik had met Bob and Anneli. We have followed their observation studies and heard the reflections that emerged from their attempts at problem-solving.

In this teacher training experiment, problem-solving was looked upon as a central concept. In Swedish universities there is much talk about 'problem-oriented learning' or 'open learning'. In both cases the learner has choice: not absolute choice, but freedom to manoeuvre. The learner will have more control than in traditional training. In 'open learning' it should be the learner who decides on the pace he or she is going to work at. Open learning also means that the learners have much control over where, when and how they study. They can learn at home, in a library, in the office or elsewhere. Lectures are kept to a minimum although the lecturer is far from unnecessary. First of all, introductory material is always presented in conventional face-to-face courses, including study guidance, aims and objectives, options of literature, laboratories, experimental devices, tuition, etc., directions for individual checking up on objectives and tutor-marked assignments.

According to Race (1989, p.17):

> The human side of open learning needs people who:
> • can be counsellors, fine-tuning the learning programme to the different needs and capabilities of learners;
> • can select the learning modules which will be most beneficial;
> • can assess learners' work on the modules;
> • can encourage and motivate learners;
> • can deal with individual problems on an individual basis.
>
> Thus, the open learning system presupposes that the learner has the feeling 'I am getting there under my own steam'.

The supporters of open learners could perhaps be called trainers, but a better term would be tutors: they can be resources, rather than 'transmitters' of information. 'Transmitting' may be all right but how 'switched on' are the student teachers as 'receivers'?

Most student teachers have reached an age when they have interests and problems which are typical of adults. Adults in teacher training often feel aliented when they start their new education. They feel bad at language, since their textbooks use a style and terminology of a very unfamiliar type. They experience difficulty in writing in the new style and terminology. They may even find research factors and concepts unpleasant. Teacher trainers should be able to understand the problems when people begin to study. They must be able to respond to the students when they feel insecure, when they say 'I do not understand a thing', when they ask, 'Will I never get to the bit I want?' or, 'Is there a need for all these prerequisites?'

This is no less important if the student teacher participates in a problem-oriented learning course. Problem-oriented learning means just what it says: problems in your future profession are starting points for your learning. One main topic could start from the question of how to organize the mathematical learning for an intellectually disabled girl of 12. Around this core theme, various sub-themes are brought together, partly 'need-to-know material', partly 'nice-to-know material'.

Problem orientation in teacher education is challenging. It makes individual assignments attractive and accommodates various interests. High-fliers benefit by being able to work at their own faster pace, particularly through introductory parts of their courses. Low-fliers can spend extra time by working through a module more than once and devote more repetition and effort to topics where at the start they had shaky knowledge. Problem-solving techniques are particularly appreciated by students who may play the part of pathfinders rather than being interested in run-of-the-mill involvement. But involvement in something new and problematic can help even run-of-the-mill teachers to become small-scale innovators.

Dangers with problem-oriented learning are, for instance, that the learner may overlook useful areas or disregard formal skills. Learners weak in language (for instance people learning in a second language) may spend too much energy and time on unnecessary trifles. Over-anxious learners may not be able to keep time and pace and so may be left behind or show too little self-confidence to risk examinations.

The tutor must assume a lot of responsibility for each student. When the problem-oriented approach is used, most learners would like some support. Even with the best planning, a good tutor can make all the difference to the student teacher's voyage. A helpful beginning is to think about the learners themselves. Some are keen to start, others need help to work on their own. Some have good study qualifications, others have limited opportunities to study or need help in learning from textbooks. It may be a good idea for the tutor to make his or her own learner profiles. The learners' need in mid-course or towards the end of a course ought to be noted. Giving students the opportunity to talk openly with the tutor can do a lot to break down barriers and to avoid disappointment.

In a scheme of this kind, the time for teaching can go down from (say) between 25 and 30 hours per week of face-to-face courses to not more than ten hours. The remaining 15 to 20 hours will be used for individual work or group sessions in laboratories, workshops, various institutions or classes. Every student follows a partly individual programme where a problem case is the core of the assignments. This problem issue should be subject to investigation and discussion by a group of students. The project carried out by Chris and Erik demonstrates the usefulness of the problem-oriented approach.

REFERENCES

Donovan, B. (1989) *Empowerment, Disability and Curriculum Development in School Mathematics*. Geelong, Victoria, Australia: Karringal East Geelong Community.
Donovan, B. (1990) 'Cultural power and the defining of school mathematics: a case study'. In T. Cooney and C.H. Hirsch (eds) *Teaching and Learning Mathematics in the 1990s* (1990 Yearbook). Reston, VA: National Council of Teachers of Mathematics.
Freire, P. (1985) *The Politics of Education: Culture, Power and Liberation*. South Hadley, MA: Bergin & Garvey.
Janke, C. (1980) 'Computational errors of mentally retarded students'. *Psychology in Schools*, **17**(1), 30–32.
Kylén, G. (1974) *Psykiskt Utvecklingshämmades Förstånd* (The Intelligence of the Mentally Retarded). Stockholm: Utbildningsförlaget.

Magne, O. and Thörn, K. (1987) 'En Kognitiv taxonomi för matematikundervisningen' ('A cognitive taxonomy for mathematics teaching'). *Psykologsk-pedagogiska Problem*. Malmö, Sweden: School of Education No. 471–2.

Mellin-Olsen, S. (1987) *The Politics of Mathematics Education*. Dordrecht: Reidel.

Nyborg, M. (1986) *En Undervisningsmodel* (A Teaching Mode). Haugesund, Norway: Norsk Spesialpedagogisk Forlag.

Race, P. (1989) *The Open Learning Handbook*. London: Kogan Page.

Part IV

Country Reports

Chapter 12

Challenges for Teacher Education: Towards Meeting Students' Special Needs from a Czech Republic Perspective

Marie Černá

DISABILITY AND CZECH SOCIETY

The Czech Republic has a long and revered history of providing for and educating citizens with mental retardation as well as a rich tradition of caring for them. The first institution for the 'feeble-minded' was established in Prague in 1871 and the first special school 15 years later in 1896. At that time the country was part of the Austro-Hungarian empire and the historical pattern paralleled the development of services for mentally retarded people found in several European countries as well as in countries overseas. In 1869 an Imperial Law ensured care for the handicapped. In 1929 an enactment stipulated that compulsory education for children with mental retardation should last eight years.

The tradition goes much further back than this. It was 400 years ago when the celebrated Czech educator Jan Amos Komenský (1592–1670), known as Comenius, brilliant thinker, philosopher and 'messenger of peace', a priest of the Community of Czech Brethren, advocated that 'backward' children were entitled to an education. 'In our orchards,' he said, 'we like to have not only trees that bring forth early fruit, but also those that are late-bearing. Why, therefore, should we wish that in the garden of letters only one class of intellects, the forward and active, should be tolerated?' (Komenský, 1937, p. 85)

The Czechs accepted Comenius's ideological heritage as a serious inspiration for adherents of different philosophical and ideological trends, including those in special education. His ideas are still living, and we can think about their influence on the twenty-first century. He stressed practical activity and creative human work as key factors in the process of reforming human life, society and the world:

> Man, furnished with will and free by nature, became the key subject of history, and a free creator with the prospect of self-realisation.
>
> Universal education became the means of reshaping the world towards harmony and humanism. It was not to be limited merely to schooling for a future profession, but was to permeate the individual's whole life.

The individual's education is a development of his natural abilities, the creation of a balance between personal freedom and social order, a process of accepting that every individual is responsible for the entire community and the community responsible for every individual member.

Universal culture and the integration of scientific disciplines are necessary for the consistent utilisation of all spiritual values for the public good and for a close link between theory and practice.

People, improved by lifelong education, were to realise universal reform and enjoy its fruits: harmony between man and nature, rational welfare, tolerance among individuals and peace among nations. (Komenský, 1937, pp. 139–40)

The Czechs are proud of Comenius, but not only of him. During the history of the nation there have been many excellent thinkers who have influenced Czech understanding towards handicapped people, as well as inspiring Czech special education, which has a rich tradition. Based on democratic principles, special education received significant attention, especially in the period between the two wars, both within the education, health and social systems and at the level of special educational theory. Professionals from various fields – medicine, education, psychology, sociology – developed special educational theory on authentic biological and philosophical bases. This interdisciplinary approach is the guiding principle in current Czech special educational theory and practice.

During the totalitarian regime we had both positive and negative experiences in special education. Proclamations and generally acceptable legislation strongly contrasted with the segregation in practice of persons with a disability and with the isolation of special education. The education of pupils with disabilities was isolated to the maximum extent, and this applied especially to those with mental retardation. By establishing institutions for people with severe disabilities far from communities, the impression was given that there were no disabled people in society.

Almost 40 years of Marxist-Leninist ideology left Czechoslovakia with a residue of concepts that focused on individual defects in special education. The recent opening up to Western ideas has exposed special education, all at once, to decades of research and innovative thinking. We can expect that it will take some time for Czech educators to filter and absorb the wealth of ideas, and then for us to see changes reflected in special educational theory and in the system of special education and its services.

Political changes have important effects on public policy for people with special needs. This policy, interrelated with the social and economic situation, also influences both the attitude of the public towards people with disabilities and the delivery of special services. Various voluntary organizations offer special services for children, young people and adults and for families with disabled children. The mass media frequently inform people about the problems of those with disabilities. But although current policy and its consequences are now more favourable for people with disabilities, there are still needs which require urgent attention. These include the need to:

- develop a positive vision of how people could lead more fulfilling lives;
- provide a policy framework to promote changes at the local level;
- promote coalitions of interest among public agencies, professional staff and relevant voluntary organizations;
- establish advisory, consultancy and training resources to support local initiatives;
- develop the partnership between professionals and parents;
- ensure normalization and integration.

After the political changes in 1989 the principle that disabled people should have the same rights as other citizens was widely agreed. Unfortunately, society is still far from translating this principle into practice. The principle of normalization needs to be adopted as the basis of a general social policy, embracing equality in education, employment possibilities, community living, social activities and so on. This has to be fully reflected in legislation. The first steps have already been taken, for example the relatively favourable legislative conditions stated in the document entitled the 'National Plan of Provisions for People with a Handicap' that was adopted by Parliament in September 1993. The National Plan determines the main tasks for the respective Ministries and other governmental bodies with a view to improving the quality of lives of people with disabilities. New legislation is being prepared, based on the National Plan. Yet, whereas in many national social and educational systems a significant gap exists between stated policy and actual practice in special education, in the Czech Republic, ironically enough, such a gap does not exist, since reform has not yet penetrated even at the level of policy.

Compared with the United States and other Western countries, the Czech Republic faces a more difficult economic situation, even if it is relatively at the best level among the post-communist countries of Central and Eastern Europe. Achieving fundamental reform will necessarily be a lengthy business. It is possible in the short term to create a more positive vision of life for people with mental and other disabilities and to demonstrate this vision through small projects; but changing the whole system is likely to require purposeful strategies over ten to twenty years. Finding ways to pursue these strategies at the same time as wider changes are occurring in social attitudes and forms of public administration probably adds both to the opportunities and the complexities of the task.

As we move towards the twenty-first century the importance of developing and implementing effective transition services for people with disabilities is clear. Despite the previous investment in services and more recent reforms, many people with special needs remain isolated. We need to be advocates for all those with disabilities; better still, we need to work with disabled adults, particularly in order to help those with mental handicaps, who were not trained as young children to undertake choices, to make decisions for themselves and assume control over their lives.

Disabled people, including those with mental handicaps, need to learn to speak for themselves on important issues such as housing, employment, legal rights and personal relationships. We also need to change the attitudes of society, to destroy the myths, false perceptions and stereotypes which surround disability. We must learn how to work together, how to develop partnerships both among professionals and between professionals and parents. Such collaboration and links between the various groups are imperative if we are to improve the quality of life for people with disabilities.

THE NEW GENERAL SITUATION IN THE FIELD OF EDUCATION

Schools, quite as much as other institutions, will have to play an active role in the radical reorganization, based on pluralist democracy and human values, which has followed the revolution of 1989. This will involve crucial change in many aspects of the school's life, specifically:

- in the position of the school in a society;
- in the prestige of schools and teachers;
- in the role of teachers in the community;
- in the systems and features of schools, including curricula, teaching and learning methods;
- in the relations between teachers and pupils;
- in the development of partnership among professionals involved in education;
- in the involvement of parents in education.

Changing schools from inside and from below is the most essential part of the current Czech effort. New educational reforms are being prepared and the first proposals of the Ministry of Education have already been published in order to ensure a broad discussion among teachers and other interested people. The strategy is a gradual one, starting from basic, so-called 'public school' children aged 6 to 11. Selected schools tested new proposals during the school year 1993–94. The proposals for public schools, while proclaiming democracy and freedom, include also the statement that 'the public school will be open to everybody, but not for those who require extra special care'. It is to be hoped that this will be changed before the proposals are accepted for enactment. Several independent bodies, such as professional groups and teacher organizations, will offer their own proposals; private and church schools will provide pupils with their own programmes. Everything is on the move, creating a new situation in the field of Czech education.

School administration and management in Czechoslovakia before November 1989 was highly centralized. It was based on the assumption that central bodies should make and provide the teacher with comprehensive, ready-made aims, curricula, methods and organizational prescriptions. Maintaining control of all the rules and demands was thought to be the best way to ensure the desired results. Yet in spite of massive supervision, this system did not function well. The effort nowadays has been to give teachers the right to make their own choices, to initiate their own solutions and changes. By this means they are to have more initiative in determining the content of curricula and in methods of teaching, and to be more responsible for the development of each pupil's personality. But the attempt to implement these measures has revealed that teachers are not well prepared for the new challenge.

It is agreed that the mission of the contemporary teacher is not merely to teach – not even only to educate individual children in a broad sense – but to accept responsibility for the economic, cultural and social development of society and for the promotion of positive human relations both inside and outside each community. Thus the activity of the teacher assumes cultural and humanistic dimensions.

TEACHER EDUCATION

There are many reasons why it is necessary to improve the quality of the Czech system of teacher education. These include the needs to make it more effective, to coordinate it with the educational reforms and to prepare teachers for the new situation. Many issues must be in focus in regard to the improvement of teacher education:

- the relationship between educational theory and school practice;
- the relationship between teaching effectiveness and school management;
- the development of teacher creativity;
- the development of teacher responsibility;
- the implementation of information technology and of new technologies in the teaching of foreign languages;
- the introduction of environmental education;
- an acceptance of the ideas of global education and internationalization;
- assessment and evaluation.

As a heritage from the past, a rift exists between family and school: the majority of teachers are afraid of parents and the majority of parents do not believe the school. Harmony and cooperation between school and family have been declared to be desirable but do not exist in practice. Cooperation from the school side focused mainly on giving parents information about the academic progress and behaviour of their child. Parents were expected to provide strong support for the school rules, to control homework and to ensure good conditions for the child's home study. The proclaimed harmony and cooperation represented in fact a subordination of the family to the aims of official education. Families were isolated, with no possibility of affecting education and school policy: they had no opportunity to express their views about this.

Generally, it is felt necessary that the situation must rapidly be changed. Parliament took the first step when it passed the Act of State Administration and Self-Government of Schools in 1992. The Act covers parents' claims as well as the claims of teachers, pupils, and other people interested in education. The partnership between school and family is a vital and urgent challenge to current Czech education. The conviction prevails that parents should play an important role in school so that they can fully exercise their rights.

SPECIAL EDUCATION ISSUES

All of these and many more problems are important and are reflected in the field of special education, especially:

- changing the public's perception of, and attitude towards, their fellow citizens with special needs;
- increasing parental involvement and participation in the education of their child with a disability;
- mandating the integration of students with special needs into mainstream academic environments;
- adopting the principles of normalization as a social policy.

One current task is the integration of disabled pupils into regular classes. This policy has generated a variety of responses from parents, teachers and administrators. While some people perceive it as being progressive and offering substantial benefits to the children concerned, others express a completely opposite point of view: the NIMBY ('not in *my* back yard') phenomenon featured in the attitude of many teachers in ordinary schools. Special school teachers are mostly afraid of losing their jobs; they argue against integration, claiming that it will not provide disabled pupils with a proper educational environment. Whatever opinion people hold, a new democratic school must offer special children learning experiences which enable them to enjoy life to the fullest.

When educating students with special needs, it is impossible to be successful without establishing a strong partnership between parents and teachers. The role of individual parents, and the parent associations, together with other voluntary organizations, becomes more important as education is changing.

The Czech Association for Help to the Mentally Handicapped is one of the advanced voluntary organizations working for the benefit of people with mental retardation. The Association has been developing its activities for 25 years, during which period it was practically shut off from the rest of the world. Due to the changes since November 1989 and the new democratic and social conditions in our country, it is no longer forbidden to develop new activities.

The Association's original mission was to bring parents of mentally handicapped children together, to provide them with relevant information about social, health and educational services, and to help them meet the individual needs of their children. The Association has also been serving as a guidance and consulting centre. It has organized many leisure activities for people with mental disabilities, including sporting events and physical education, dancing lessons, swimming, skiing and other recreational activities. A great boom in the Association's activity came after 1989: the number of members increased roughly ten times and the Association established 12 facilities for children and adults with mental retardation, which provide clients with modern educational and social services as well as individual support.

Another interesting example of innovation is a small-scale project, the Night School for Mentally Handicapped Adults. It is run by the Psychopedics Association, an organization of professionals working in the field of mental retardation. Its mission is to support the professional development of all the Association's members, who in different places can contribute to the lives of people with mental retardation. A group of professionals, especially special school teachers, started the Association's activity in 1982, but the independent organization was founded in Prague in 1990.

Nowadays the Association has over 500 members in the Czech Republic, and more than 150 foreign members from many countries. The majority of its members are teachers at special schools and institutions for mentally handicapped people; some are researchers, university teachers and other professionals enthusiastic about the Association's programme. This focuses on sharing ideas in special education theory and in the implementation of new experiences in special services and support for people with mental retardation. The Association regularly organizes seminars, conferences and discussion groups. In September 1991 the Night School also opened, offering further education courses for mentally handicapped adults. The students, all over 18, are leavers from special schools or those who were excluded from obligatory school attendance during their school age but who can benefit from further education. The work with these students is rewarding: it is clear that education enhances the lives of the students and contributes to their integration in the community.

CURRENT DIRECTIONS IN SPECIAL EDUCATION

Integration, normalization and ideas related to these are the current topics in Czech special education. Education of disabled children was extremely isolated in Czechoslovakia during the communist period. By establishing special institutions for persons with severe disabilities far from communities, it looked as if there were no disabled people in the society. For reasons of ideology, the government wanted it to appear as if everybody was happy in a socialist country.

Since 1989 it has been recognized that the right to equality in education is a right that should be accorded to disabled people and their families; we are sure that we shall only make progress if we continue to insist on this basic right for all children with disabilities, including their right to integrated education. Not to do this would be to accept second-class citizenship for disabled people, for families with a disabled child, and for the professionals who work with them.

The major challenge of special education today is both to meet the ordinary needs of all children as children, and at the same time to meet any special needs that arise from their disabilities. From that viewpoint, many tasks remain for special education in the Czech Republic, for example early detection and evaluation, early intervention, the development of individual educational plans, the setting of short-term teaching targets, cooperative work with parents, and the use of natural teaching situations.

The first priority for school-age disabled children is to ensure that they have access to schools at all. This is a matter of rights and legislation. Next there is integration, which as we have seen involves many problems. Many teachers and even some parents are not committed to integration. They are worried about dismantling hundreds of special schools and institutions and dispersing the children and the staff into ordinary schools. Resistance to change is understandable when a tried system for provision of services is being replaced by the unknown. Therefore integration is also progressing step by step, starting with kindergarten projects. Integration is more and more the central issue of special education and, indeed, of education itself.

One way to prepare better conditions for integration is through teacher education. This plays a significant role in the professionalism of the teacher's activity. The professionalism of the teacher means in essence humanism, and is reflected in a number of skills and characteristics: in the capacity to evaluate the educational process objectively and analyse its effectiveness; to generalize acquired experience and compare it with knowledge of educational theory; to establish and maintain optimal pedagogical communication; to motivate the pupil to the desired activity; to support the development of student activity; to create a favourable emotional atmosphere; to prevent the development of a psychological barrier which makes it impossible for pupils with special needs to use their capacity to the maximum extent. Developing real professionalism in teachers is important: only a professional-humanist teacher will respond to the growing demands of an ever more democratic society.

Teachers can also profit from disabled pupils. On the basis of systematic, planned and purposeful activity, teachers gradually enrich their professionalism, improve the methods they use, enlarge their pedagogical horizon and the spectrum of their educational impact. In fact we can say that both the theory and practice of the educational process are being improved. If teachers want to be successful, they must constantly correct, modify and adapt their activity with regard to both the long-standing and current needs of the disabled child. In order to be able to achieve this, their knowledge base must continue to grow, so they must study and educate themselves on a lifelong basis. In the dynamics of a life-educational process, their professionalism improves, including the development and refinement of adequate attitudes towards each child to be educated.

Disabled pupils teach their teachers many things, especially how

- to pretend nothing;
- to give a person the right to be different;
- to enjoy happiness;
- to promote efforts aimed at a good cause;
- to give a higher appreciation to the moral qualities of the individual;
- to respect parents;
- to notice lesser achievements as well;
- to assess people with regard to their relation to those with special needs.

The last of these items relates particularly to the current situation in my country. A lot has been said about the need to assess the level of a society's development by reference to the care it provides for its disabled persons. Similarly, the relation of individuals towards disabled people should be one criterion of the value of their personality. It is not unusual to admire and be fond of a healthy child and do everything for his or her welfare. However, giving disabled people the same right to happiness and love as others enjoy is far from being natural, yet. It is our obligation to the disabled children and their families which the humanistic teacher will help us fulfil.

REFERENCES AND FURTHER READING

Gargiulo, R. and Černá, M. (1992a) 'Special education in Czechoslovakia: characteristics and issues'. *International Journal of Special Education*, **7**(1), 60–70.
Gargiulo, R. and Černá, M. (1992b) 'Perspectives on mental retardation in Czechoslovakia'. *European Journal of Special Needs Education*, **7**(3), 219–28.
Komenský, J.A. (Comenius) (1937) *Didaktika Česká*. Prague: I.L. Kober.
Pánek, J. (1991) *Joan Amos Comenius*. Kosice, Prague: Orbis.
Philpott, T. (1990) 'Out of sight, out of mind'. *Community Care*, 22 November, 16–19.
Sovák, M. (1984) *Introduction to Special Education*. Prague: State Educational Publishing House.

Chapter 13

Professional Development for Special Needs Education in England and Wales

Peter Mittler

INTRODUCTION

The concept of special educational needs in the United Kingdom comprises an average of 20 per cent of all children and is far broader than the 1.5 per cent of children in special schools. More than half of all children who are thought to require 'additional provision' and are given 'statements' of special educational need under the 1981 and 1993 Acts are now in ordinary schools.

Since every teacher is by definition working with pupils with special educational needs, the professional development needs of such teachers are by definition inseparable from those of all teachers. It follows that the training and education of all teachers must include an introduction to the needs of such pupils and ways in which they may be met in ordinary schools.

The needs of children with special educational needs overlap with those of an even larger group of 'low-achieving' or 'underachieving' children, most of whom come from socially and economically disadvantaged backgrounds. The relationship between social disadvantage and educational attainment seems to have become almost a taboo subject in polite educational circles. But it represents a major challenge for educational planning, classroom practice and teacher education (Mittler, 1993a).

IMPLICATIONS OF NEW LEGISLATION FOR TRAINING

A new *Code of Practice on the Assessment and Identification of Special Educational Needs* (Department for Education, 1993) sets out clear expectations of ways in which all ordinary schools are expected to identify, assess and meet the needs of pupils with learning or behavioural difficulties. Every school is required to develop a clear special needs policy statement, to appoint a special needs coordinator and to 'have regard to' the guidelines in the Code of Practice on procedures for early identification and intervention.

The implications of the Code of Practice for teacher training are that all teachers must have basic competencies in special needs education and that those with designated responsibilities for working with pupils with SEN will need additional skills. This includes all school SEN coordinators (SENCOs), members of learning support teams within schools, as well as peripatetic teams of support teachers employed by the local education authority or other agencies. It also includes all teachers working in special schools and in special classes and units in ordinary schools.

The Code of Practice has been well received because, for the first time, detailed guidance is given on ways in which ordinary schools should not only identify but seek to meet special needs at an early stage. But their implications for teacher education have so far not been adequately recognized by the government. If children who require 'additional provision beyond that which is generally available' are eligible for additional resources, those who teach them should also have access to additional training to equip and support them in this task. This calls for a radical reappraisal of the whole of initial and post-experience training for all teachers but particularly those with specific responsibilities for working with pupils with special educational needs.

INITIAL TEACHER EDUCATION

All courses of initial teacher education (ITE) have for some time been required to include an SEN element to ensure that all new teachers have some degree of awareness of how children with SEN can be identified and supported in gaining access to the curriculum. Training institutions were inspected by Her Majesty's Inspectorate (HMI) to ensure compliance with these requirements. A summary of these requirements and an account of the difficulties experienced in implementing them was published in 1992 (Mittler, 1992; discussed in greater detail in Mittler, 1993a) but these accounts have now been overtaken by new legislation and new challenges.

An Education Act was approved by Parliament in 1994, after much debate inside and outside Parliament. This Act removed the control and funding of all initial teacher training courses from the Higher Education Funding Council and vested it in a new Teacher Training Agency (TTA) that was established in September 1994.

In addition, the government has made it clear that it would like to increase the proportion of time which teacher training students spend in schools from the present norm of around 67 per cent in secondary training to as much as 100 per cent in some cases. Schools are being encouraged to set up consortia in order to accept full responsibility for initial teacher training and will be provided with the fees which would normally go to the training institution. They are allowed to offer such training without the support of higher education, if that is their choice. But they can also contract with higher education to provide certain elements of training.

But how will universities or schools (with or without university input) be able to provide an adequate SEN element in future, now that an increasing proportion of training will be school based? It is not enough to observe 'good SEN practice' in schools, even where it exists (and HMI reports suggest that good practice is not all that common). Students need opportunities to read and think critically about what constitutes good practice and to be exposed to staff with interests and experience in this area.

It is not clear how the time can be found for universities to continue to provide a special needs element in initial training or how schools can do so on their own. Students undertaking their training in schools will be entirely dependent on the quality of special needs provision in those schools. Since HMI and research reports are critical of the quality of such provision at the present time, it is hard to have confidence in the new arrangements. It also remains to be seen whether the new Teacher Training Agency will ensure that all training courses develop a special needs element.

At Manchester University, a 'special needs pack' has been written as an exercise in a version of 'distance education' for secondary students who will have only limited courses with their tutors in a 36-week course, only 12 of which will be spent in the university (Farrell, 1993). The pack includes specific tasks and exercises for them to follow during the PGCE course, as well as introductory notes and materials. In addition, all students are still required to spend two weeks in a special needs placement.

The new proposals differ radically from existing practice, which is based on a real partnership between schools and higher education, with a much greater role than in the past being played by schools in the selection of students and in training in classroom and pedagogic skills.

Three complementary approaches to providing the SEN element in initial teacher training have been identified (Mittler, 1992):

- *permeation*, in which a special needs element is included as an integral element of all theoretical and practical courses and experiences;
- *focused*, in which attention is concentrated on special needs issues during a course of lectures, seminars or practical experiences;
- *optional*, in which students have an opportunity to study aspects of special needs practice in greater depth.

An evaluation by HMI (1990) drew attention to the problems of relying too much on the 'permeation' approach delivered by mainstream ITE tutors and stressed the need for both 'focused' and 'optional' elements provided by specialist tutors. A detailed report and guidelines were also prepared by the Council for National Academic Awards (1991), a body which validated all teacher education courses in the public sector but which has since been abolished. Despite these courses, the HMI surveys of the *New Teacher in School* (e.g. OFSTED, 1993a) regularly report that new teachers feel inadequately prepared to teach low-achieving children.

CONTINUING PROFESSIONAL DEVELOPMENT

Given the problems of providing an adequate SEN element to ITE students, what are the prospects of doing so within the framework of continuing professional development?

Induction

With the abolition of the probationary period, it is more than ever important that the process of induction, whether provided by schools or LEAs, should pay particular attention to ways of supporting new teachers in working with pupils with SEN. A report on induction by HMI (1992a) suggests that this is not receiving enough attention. Now that universities are becoming more involved in supporting induction, there is an opportunity to ensure that SEN issues are addressed.

Government grants for in-service training

Up to the early 1980s, government funding for post-experience training was provided from a central pool of funds.

In 1983, special needs was one of only four initial priorities identified by the Department of Education and Science in its scheme of earmarked in-service funding, then totalling around £7 million. The total sum available for 1993–94 was £320 million of which 60 per cent was provided by the Department, with the balance to be found by LEAs. The sum of £10 million is available for all SEN training, compared with £180 million for training on National Curriculum, assessment and information technology.

During the early 1980s, SEN training funds were allocated to specific national SEN priorities. These included one-term courses for designated teachers in ordinary schools (SENIOS course), post-experience qualifying courses for teachers of hearing-impaired and visually impaired children (for which there is still a mandatory requirement) and courses for teachers of children with severe learning difficulties, as well as professional training for educational psychologists. Other areas were regarded as 'local priorities' for which LEAs had to assume a greater share of the costs.

At first, the earmarking of training funds and the setting of national and local priorities had a beneficial effect, since it was designed to encourage a planned approach to the identification of staff development needs at the level of the LEA, the school and individual members of staff. From the mid-1980s, however, what started as a promising government initiative has disintegrated in response to lack of LEA resources, both human and financial.

Furthermore, the policy of delegating budgets to schools, while welcome in some respects, has left little or no money for staff development. Certainly, the sums available make it impossible for schools to second a staff member for advanced courses, even on a part-time basis. In addition to the cost of fees, schools still have to find the replacement costs of teachers absent from school on training courses even for one day.

The Department for Education (DfE) has since exacerbated the problem by providing only a lump sum for all SEN training and abolishing funding for local priorities altogether, leaving LEAs and schools to determine their own priorities. As a result, many of the one-term SENIOS courses as well as full-time and part-time courses for specialist teachers of sensorily and intellectually impaired children are undersubscribed and becoming unviable. The only exception is a small sum earmarked for courses of teachers of 'deaf/blind' children, an exception almost certainly due to persistent lobbying by the appropriate voluntary organizations.

We have a major crisis of teacher supply on our hands which the government has until now steadfastly refused to acknowledge. This arises in large measure from the decision made in 1985 to phase out specialist initial training courses for students wishing to work with children with sensory or intellectual impairments.

An HMI (1992b) national report shows that in 1986 over 200 new teachers from 11 four-year full time B.Ed. courses qualified to work with pupils with severe learning difficulties. By 1991, only 35 new entrants qualified by an in-service route and it was estimated that only 15 teachers would gain a specialist qualification in this field in 1994. Similarly, only 101 teachers obtained a specialist qualification in the education of hearing-impaired children in 1992, compared to the officially estimated target of between 140 and 160 needed to replace normal losses.

The same survey provides information on virtually all the specialist award-bearing courses available in the field of hearing impairment (HI), visual impairment (VI) and severe learning difficulties. It reaches the following conclusions:

- All HI and VI and three-quarters of SLD courses provided satisfactory or better training and preparation. The standard of teaching was generally good.
- All VI courses had recruited their full numbers but recruitment to HI courses had fallen by 20 per cent in two years.
- Eight of the 12 SLD courses were undersubscribed and most of their course members were already teaching in SLD schools. The majority of students were over 35, with over ten years' previous teaching experience.

A separate national review of all government-supported training carried out by HMI between April 1991 and April 1992 specifically noted the low priority given in ordinary schools to training in the field of special educational needs (OFSTED, 1993a).

OPPORTUNITIES FOR MORE EXPERIENCED TEACHERS

As initial teacher education moves increasingly out of higher education and into schools, opportunities for continuing professional development for all teachers become even more important.

The story of the gradual attrition of opportunities for teachers to study for award-bearing courses is too well known to require retelling. What has not emerged, however, is a coherent policy for staff development for teachers. Long courses have been replaced by a large number of short one-day training events, mostly based in schools and delivered by other teachers and by advisers. A large number of training days have been directly targeted on the National Curriculum and the assessment arrangements. These include the five days a year 'non-contact days' which can be devoted to training, usually within the school. At the same time, the advent of modularization has further eroded opportunities for specialization. Most diplomas and master's degree courses are now 'generic' rather than categorical. While this has undoubted advantages in laying broader foundations in special needs issues 'across the board', the advent of modular courses makes it difficult to assess the extent to which teachers have made a detailed and in-depth study of one or more areas of special needs provision.

In the past, proposals for new award-bearing courses had to be approved by the Department of Education and Science, who usually sought the advice of HMI who in turn provided helpful and constructive advice – for example on the content of the course, the balance between theory and practice, aims, objectives and methods. Such quality control is no longer available, partly because the size of the Inspectorate has been drastically reduced and partly because those who are left are largely concerned with school inspection.

Distance education

Another response of universities to the gradual disappearance of one-year full-time courses has taken the form of the production of distance education courses. Patricia Potts (Chapter 2 in this volume) describes the well established and highly successful work of the Open University which has been active in this field for over 20 years. Other universities are also producing distance education versions of their existing diploma and master's modules. Some of these distance courses are designed for use within the UK itself, particularly for teachers working with visually and hearing-impaired pupils and those with severe learning difficulties. Others are designed for students working overseas, particularly those in developing countries.

Training designated teachers in ordinary schools

A welcome and successful initiative took the form of one-term courses specifically for 'teachers with designated responsibilities for pupils with SENs in ordinary schools'. With the aim of helping experienced teachers to become agents of change in their own school, course members typically spent three days in higher education and two days back in their own schools. By 1986, 25 such courses were running and even in 1988 the DES was expecting all teachers with designated SEN responsibilities to undergo such training eventually. The planning and delivery of the courses provided opportunities for a distinctive partnership between higher education, an LEA adviser, the head-teacher and the seconded teacher. The students were supported in the development of a whole-school approach and in the management of change.

An independent evaluation by the National Foundation for Educational Research (Hegarty and Hodgson, 1988) of these 25 one-term SENIOS courses suggested that they had a considerable impact on schools, particularly where the headteachers were already committed to change and where management of change was well planned and resourced. The report provides many examples of innovations which could be directly attributed to the courses.

Given this promising start, it is a great pity that these courses are now withering on the vine, due largely to the inability of LEAs to fund their share of the costs. Some of the courses are now taught on the basis of one half-day or evening a week, but with greatly depleted numbers. The partnership with LEAs has eroded with the disappearance of specialist advisers and the demands of inspection.

Opportunities for support teachers

One of the distinctive features of special needs practice in the UK can be found in the work of peripatetic teams of teachers who visit groups of schools in order to support teachers working with pupils with special educational needs. Learning support teams have until now been based on and funded by LEAs; some areas of specialization have been developed, such as support of children with sensory or physical impairments or pupils with emotional or behavioural difficulties or those with specific learning difficulties The work of these teams complements that of teachers in mainstream schools with designated responsibilities for pupils with SEN.

With the devolution of funding to schools and a reduced role for the LEA, there are uncertainties about how support services are to be funded in the future and the extent to which schools will wish to pay for their services. But if support services are to remain an LEA responsibility, how and from whom will they receive further training? What should be the content of courses? It is obviously vital that support teachers should have access to courses which are related to their distinctive needs over and above those available to all teachers. In particular, they need preparation and support in respect of their consultancy and negotiation roles and in the skills involved in working with other adults, including those in senior management positions whose support for their work is vital.

A detailed report by Blythman (1985) documents the development of a nationwide diploma in learning difficulties in Scotland; 40 per cent of the course content was specifically concerned with preparation for such consultancy and support work in ordinary schools.

Staff of special schools

Staff working in special schools include not only teachers but nursery nurses and classroom assistants, now collectively known as special support assistants. In addition, there is a need for joint courses with speech therapists and physiotherapists and other health practitioners such as doctors and nurses, as well as educational psychologists, educational social workers, careers officers and specialist advisory teachers and curriculum specialists. There is a strong argument for much more joint training, not only with other professionals but also with governors and parents.

Traditionally, teachers in special schools had access to a wide range of full-time diploma and master's courses, or their part-time equivalents. Some of these provided mandatory qualifications. But recruitment to these courses dropped by two-thirds in a single year, as a direct result of the funding changes introduced by the government around 1986. The training imperatives introduced by the 1988 Education Reform Act, the introduction of the 'non-contact' days and the need for short school-based and skill-based courses marked the demise of the long course in its traditional form. As a result, hardly any teachers now have the opportunity to undertake an advanced course leading to a diploma or master's or research degree, even on a part-time basis. As a nation, we are failing to provide advanced courses of professional development and research training for the next generation of teachers.

In addition to training in all aspects of the National Curriculum, assessment arrangements, individual planning, financial management, etc., teachers in special schools also require support in working with colleagues in ordinary schools and in promoting, managing and above all sustaining change in both special and ordinary schools. They have much to contribute to their colleagues in ordinary schools in relation to curriculum planning and modification, devising a small-steps approach to helping pupils access the programmes of study and attainment targets of the National Curriculum assessment and record-keeping, individual educational planning, behavioural methods and management, aspects of microtechnology and working with parents. They also have much to teach each other about ways of supporting integration, the obstacles encountered and how these might be overcome. At the same time, they themselves will need support in adult learning, consultancy and negotiating skills and in familiarizing themselves with the many changes which are taking place in primary and secondary schools.

Evaluation of diploma courses

Although it is unlikely that such courses will be reinstated, it is worth noting the results of a national evaluation of all specialist diploma courses being provided by higher education in 1984–85, carried out by the National Foundation for Educational Research, the last year in which such courses were provided in their traditional form.

This is provided in a full report by Dust (1988). The study involved 46 training institutions providing 37 full-time and 37 part-time courses for a total of 636 students, of whom half were from special and half from ordinary schools. Fifty-nine courses were generic, covering several areas of specific SEN, including those encountered in ordinary schools. Data were obtained from 102 tutors, 99 of whom had experience of teaching in ordinary as well as special schools and were also involved in initial teacher education in higher education.

Dust's evaluation provides a detailed analysis of the content of the courses, including theory and practice and the extent to which they sought to prepare students to manage and sustain change in their own schools. Most students have placement experiences in a range of schools other than their own. Unfortunately, no information is provided on the extent to which what was learned on the course had an impact on the teachers, the schools or the pupils they taught.

CONTEXTS FOR CHANGE

Despite this sad catalogue of failed initiatives and missed opportunities, there are nevertheless a number of sources of positive pressures for change which could result in more clearly articulated demands for staff development.

National contexts

- The 1993 Education Act requires every ordinary school to develop, implement and publicize its special needs policy and practice. The names of all staff with responsibilities for pupils with SEN also need to be listed.
- Inspections of SEN provision in both ordinary and special schools by the Office for Standards in Education (OFSTED), which has replaced HMI as the new Inspectorate, will include an assessment of the extent to which schools plan and provide for staff development. These and other inspections will in turn identify staff development needs and generate demand for relevant courses.

'Recognized' and 'mandatory' qualifications

The recommendation for a mandatory qualification for all teachers with a 'defined responsibility for children with SEN' was made as long ago as 1954 but is still far from implementation, except for teachers working in schools and units for children with sensory impairments who must gain a relevant specialist qualification within three years.

For all other teachers, a decision in principle needs to be taken about the definition and status of 'recognized qualifications' in special needs education. Clearly, there is a strong case that all teachers with significant responsibilities for pupils with special educational needs should have an 'appropriate' qualification.

For most teachers, this will in practice consist of a number of modules concerned with special needs education and may lead to an award which reflects the emphasis of the course of study as a whole on special educational needs. But many teachers may be studying for a general diploma or master's course which provides a wide range of student choice of modules, including one or two in special needs. It is a moot point whether such generic courses with only a small special needs component can be regarded as a 'recognized' qualification in special educational needs, unless, for example, a dissertation or other evidence of specialization in this area is also included.

RESEARCH

Research in special needs has not been well supported since the mid-1980s, when the government funded three major projects in SEN provision from the National Foundation for Educational Research and the Universities of London and Manchester. One of these (Robson *et al.*, 1988) and part of a second (Hegarty and Moses, 1988) were specifically concerned with teacher education. These projects developed a range of approaches for evaluating the effectiveness of courses, including case studies, interviews and questionnaires. Brief reference has also been made to evaluations of staff development initiatives; a useful summary has been edited by Upton (1991), updating an earlier compendium by Sayer and Jones (1985).

Despite the lack of interest in funding, disseminating or using research, universities can still make a significant contribution by providing support and supervision to teachers and students who wish to undertake their own investigations (Vulliamy and Webb, 1992; O'Hanlon, 1992). By this means, the tradition of critical evaluation and impartial enquiry may be kept alive at a time when it appears to be under threat.

CONCLUSIONS

It is essential that all professional staff with a responsibility for meeting the needs of pupils with special educational needs should have access to opportunities to update their knowledge, skills and experience. The argument of this chapter has been that such opportunities have been undermined rather than enhanced and that such training as has been available has been *ad hoc* and short term. Nevertheless, despite problems of funding and the reduced role of LEAs, there is a more urgent need than ever to develop a strategic approach to staff development in special schools, classes and support services. This can be achieved through clusters of schools working together and sharing ideas and resources.

The implementation of the Code of Practice and the 1993 Education Act, as well as other legislation such as the 1989 Children Act, requires a massive programme of staff development. This needs to provide relevant and appropriate courses for all levels of staff, from newly qualified teachers to all teachers in the system, including headteachers of all our schools, principals and senior staff of colleges of further education, members of support services, educational psychologists, school governors, staff of health and social service departments and voluntary organizations. The first priority should be the special needs coordinators which are required in every school (Mittler, 1994).

There is now a lively debate on the nature and level of the knowledge, skills and understanding required of all teachers in the system, but especially those with clearly designated and sometimes specific responsibilities for pupils with special educational needs. At the time of writing, it is not clear whether the government itself will provide leadership in this area – for example by setting up a staff development study group which will make recommendations – or whether it will commission others to do so.

The matter is too urgent and the crisis of teacher education too acute to justify further delay. The time is ripe for action.

REFERENCES

Blythman, M. (1985) 'National initiatives: the Scottish experience'. In J. Sayer and N. Jones (eds) *Teacher Training and Special Educational Needs*. London: Croom Helm.

Council for National Academic Awards (1991) *Review of Special Educational Needs in Initial and In-service Teacher Education Courses*. London: CNAA.

Department for Education (1993) *Code of Practice on the Identification and Assessment of Special Educational Needs*. London: DfE.

Dust, K. (1988) 'The diploma courses'. In S. Hegarty and D. Moses (eds) *Developing Expertise: Inset for Special Educational Needs*. Windsor: NFER-Nelson.

Farrell, P. (1993) 'A special needs resource pack for secondary PGCE students'. School of Education, University of Manchester (unpublished).

Hegarty, S. and Hodgson, A. (1988) 'The one term courses'. In S. Hegarty and D. Moses (eds) *Developing Expertise: Inset for Special Educational Needs*. Windsor: NFER-Nelson.

Hegarty, S. and Moses, D. (eds) (1988) *Developing Expertise: Inset for Special Educational Needs*. Windsor: NFER-Nelson.

HMI (1990) *Special Educational Needs in Initial Teacher Training*. London: DES.

HMI (1992a) *The Induction and Probation of New Teachers*. London: DES.

HMI (1992b) *Survey Inspections of Specialist Training Courses in England and Wales for Teachers Intending to Teach Hearing-Impaired Pupils, Visually Impaired Pupils and Pupils with Severe Learning Difficulties. (1990–1991)*. London: DES.

Mittler, P. (1992) 'Preparing all initial teacher training students to teach children with special educational needs: a case study from England'. *European Journal of Special Needs Education*, **7**, 1–10.

Mittler, P. (1993a) 'Children with special educational needs'. In G. Verma and P. Pumfrey (eds) *Cross-Curricular Contexts: Themes and Dimensions in Secondary Schools*. London: Falmer Press.

Mittler, P. (1993b) *Teacher Education for Special Educational Needs*. Policy Options Paper 3. Stafford: National Association for Special Educational Needs.

Mittler, P. (1994) 'A post-code address'. *Times Educational Supplement*, 13 May. p. 21.

OFSTED (1993a) *The New Teacher in School: 1992*. London: OFSTED.

OFSTED (1993b) *The Management and Provision of In-service Training Funded by the Grant for Education and Support* London: OFSTED.

O'Hanlon, C. (1992) 'Action research in special education'. *European Journal of Special Needs Education*, **7**, 204–18.

Robson, C., Sebba, J., Mittler, P. and Davies, G. (1988) *In-service Training and Special Educational Needs: Running Short, School-Focused Courses*. Manchester: Manchester University Press.

Sayer, J. and Jones, N. (eds) (1985) *Teacher Training and Special Educational Needs*. London: Croom Helm.

Upton, G. (1991) 'Issues and trends in staff training'. In G. Upton (ed.) *Teacher Training and Special Educational Needs*. London: Fulton.

Vulliamy, G. and Webb, R. (eds) (1992) *Teacher Research and Special Educational Needs*. London: Fulton.

ACKNOWLEDGEMENT

This chapter is a shortened and updated version of a longer discussion paper, *Teacher Education for Special Educational Needs*, prepared for the series Policy Options for Special Educational Needs in the 1990s, published in 1993 by the National Association for Special Educational Needs and reproduced here with their permission.

Chapter 14

Special Education and Teacher Training in Hungary

Yvonne Csányi

SPECIAL EDUCATION IN HUNGARY

There exists in Hungary a more or less parallel educational system beside the regular one, a quite well organized network of special educational schools and institutes. This network was built up mainly in the last century – the first institute of special education was founded in 1802 for deaf children – but it has been growing until recently. The idea of integration or inclusive schooling is present in theory and in certain experimental models only.

The regular school system involves pre-schools that accept about 90 per cent of the children aged between 3 and 6 or 7, and compulsory schools for children from 6 or 7 to 14, or at the latest 16 years. Continuing education in vocational schools (three years) or secondary schools (four years) is optional. Since the political changes there are new types of secondary school that accept children after the fourth or sixth class of the compulsory school. Most schools are owned by the state, but some belong to churches or other foundations. The school policy in the latter schools is much more flexible than in the state schools. The national curriculum is still the old one, as there has been a disagreement over the new ideas of the last four years. The new government promises a quick solution to this problem.

The network of schools is divided into the following different types according to the area of handicap (disability): mildly mentally handicapped (or, using the new term, children with learning disabilities), moderately mentally handicapped, deaf, partially hearing, blind, partially sighted, physically handicapped, children with speech problems, and the different types of multi-handicaps. Each school type has its own officially prescribed curriculum. Acceptance of a child in a special class or school follows an official procedure in which the child is assessed by a team (medical, psychological, special educational) of the so-called 'transferring committee'.

Special pre-schools are part of the special school system. They accept children from the age of 3, and special schools accept them from the age of 6 or 7 until 14 or 16, just like the regular pre-schools and schools. The time of schooling takes one or two more years than in the regular schools, the final certificate having the same value as that

Table 14.1 *Handicapped children in special pre-schools* *

	Mentally handicapped	Hearing impaired	Sight impaired	Physically handicapped
Number of children	520	169	22	125

* Special pre-schools are attached to special schools and provide education for various categories of disabled children (as above).

Table 14.2 *Special schools or classes for handicapped children.*

	Mentally handicapped	Deaf	Partially hearing	Blind	Partially sighted	Physically handicapped
Classes	1037	-	-	-	-	-
Schools	166	7	1	1	2	2

Table 14.3 *Handicapped children in special schools or classes*

	Mentally handicapped	Deaf	Partially hearing	Blind	Partially sighted	Physically handicapped
In classes	11,136	-	-	-	-	-
In schools	20,707	483	326	70	255	231

which ordinary pupils attain after leaving the primary school at the age of 8. Most of the special schools are residential, the children going home every weekend. The qualified special teachers work with one group of children at a time, one in the morning and another in the afternoon. There is a shortage of qualified special teachers in classes and schools for mildly mentally handicapped children; about 60 per cent of the teachers have no qualification except for regular schools. According to the new educational law this situation has to be changed within the next five years. For mildly mentally handicapped children there are also classes other than those in the separate special schools; these are usually attached to regular schools in villages or small towns. This does not, however, imply integration and is not accepted as a good solution, since the teachers are not qualified and there is a lack of resources.

Some figures, from the official statistical data for 1992–93 of the Hungarian Ministry of Education, are presented in Tables 14.1–14.3. These figures comprise 2.6 per cent of the 6- to 15-year-old population (learning disabled and mentally handicapped 2.45 per cent; hearing impaired 0.08 per cent; visually impaired 0.04 per cent; physically handicapped 0.03 per cent). To them must be added the children in the Peto Institute in Budapest (246) and the children with speech problems. There exist two schools for speech-impaired children who attend for one or more years (160 pupils), and a network of outpatient clinics taking care of about 40,000 children of pre-school and school age.

The number of *multi-handicapped* children, who have mental retardation together with a sensory or physical handicap, has been growing. They are in special schools or classes attached to a special school. Of these children, 97 are partially hearing, 127 are deaf, 81 are blind and 16 partially sighted. There are also children with *more severe handicaps*, who stay at home and receive individual support of six hours a week; there are 546 of these children. Multi-handicapped and mentally retarded adolescents have certain opportunities to continue their studies in *special vocational classes or schools*. There are not enough placements of this kind to meet the demand; at present 3645 mentally retarded young people enjoy this facility, 18 with hearing impairments and 7 who are visually impaired.

THE ROLE OF PARENTS

Parents' associations have been organized only during and since the political changes in Hungary. There are associations for parents of mentally retarded children and young people, of children with dyslexia (two associations), of children with hearing impairment, and of autistic children. These are usually rather small groups of parents living in the capital or in bigger cities. They have established foundations, hold regular meetings and sometimes edit newsletters. Their main aims are better learning conditions, the right for their children to be placed in regular schools, vocational training, employment opportunities and so on. One of the most severe problems is the care of adult mentally handicapped and multi-handicapped or severely disabled persons. A great number of parents have to cope with this problem alone. Parents are unaccustomed to fighting for the rights of their children; these parents' groups are therefore the exception. Parents still have to learn to work together as partners with the teachers and to play an active role in the education and care of their children.

The Hungarian education system is still in a period of transition. Teacher trainers and the leading figures in public education have a great wealth of information, and hopefully they will work out certain new methods while preserving the values of the former decades. We can only hope that the necessary basic resources will be available in future years to achieve at least the most important goals.

TEACHER TRAINING FOR SPECIAL EDUCATION

In 1900 special teacher training programmes were consolidated by the state under the title 'College Course for Teachers of Special Education'. At that time the length of training was two years, but this was increased to three years in 1924, and four years later to four years. The Bárczi Gusztáv College for Special Teacher Training and Social Work has been a completely independent institution since 1946. It is the only one of its kind in Hungary.

The areas of study

Between 1900 and 1968 training for future teachers was comprehensive. Special education teachers were trained to deal with all forms of disabilities. In 1968 the decision was made to break the programmes down into distinct disciplines and courses of study. The college has been progressively extending its fields, to include the training of 'social administrators' (1972), and from 1990 the training of social workers.

The structure of education

Special teacher education offers a full-time four-year course. Requirements for under-graduate study include successful completion of secondary school and of the college entrance examination. The minimum time for completion of the degree is four years (eight semesters).

Areas of study include the education of children with mental retardation, hearing impairment, visual impairment, speech and language difficulties requiring therapy, physical disability and behavioural problems. The students major in teaching and working with mentally retarded persons and choose a secondary subject in another area.

The phases of training

There are three phases of training:

1. General basic instruction (anatomy, pathology, psychology, linguistics, pedagogy, philosophy);
2. Professional training in two fields (applied pathology, applied psychology and diagnostics, applied teaching methods, history of special education and rehabilitation according to the special areas) in two fields (visually impaired, mentally disabled, speech and language impaired, etc.);
3. Further specialization. The content of training is divided into two parts: (1) preparation for classroom teaching for the teacher, and (2) tasks outside the classroom such as individual therapies, support services for integrated pupils, free time activities, early education for the therapist.

The ratio of theory to practice is 60 per cent to 40 per cent. Most of the college courses are held in the form of lectures and seminars. Students learn about their intended fields through seminars. There are many opportunities for students to observe and analyse classroom and therapeutic situations and to be involved in their chosen profession while in school (serial practice, six to eight hours per week; block practice for two weeks in both areas). Internship teaching for students is organized through the four field work centres which are part of the College.

Requirements

The requirements for receiving a degree are a written and successfully defended diploma project (thesis) and a pass grade in the state examination. Requirements for graduation are a diploma project, a one-lesson final teaching practice and the state examination.

The faculty and the student body

The College has ten departments and an Institute of Psychology for Special Education with an outpatient clinic for the diagnostics and therapy of disabled children. The College has 84 full-time professors and a large number of part-time lecturers.

The student body is responsible for decisions relating to students' rights and interests (scholarships, grants, etc.), and sends representatives (30 per cent) to the highest decision-making body of the College, the College Board, and to other permanent groups. The number of undergraduate students in the initial programme is 1200, and about 300 are involved in the in-service programme.

In-service training

Eligibility for part-time study (by correspondence) is based on the students' current employment in a related field. There are two options for in-service training. The first carries the same requirements as the full-time programme. The second option differs in time requirement since the student must currently be a pre-school or school teacher. The minimum time for the completion of part-time studies is two years (four semesters).

RESEARCH

A large number of staff members have been involved in various research projects. Successful bids for grants provide financial support for the implementation of new ideas, for elaborating new programmes and for testing new technical equipment. We have projects at present sponsored by the World Bank and by the European Union in the framework of the TEMPUS/PHARE programme. One of the TEMPUS programmes of our College deals with special educational needs in the mainstream (inclusive schools), in which we act as both coordinator and contractor. In this programme we have as partners the Budapest Teacher Training College, Manchester and Cambridge Universities in England, the Heidelberg Pädagogische Hochschule in Germany and the Instituut voor Doven (a school for the deaf where in-service training is also provided), Sint Michielsgestel, the Netherlands.

REVISION OF THE TEACHER EDUCATION PROGRAMME

The teacher education programme has been revised as from the academic year 1992–93 as follows:

- Students may choose their required areas (there is no compulsory field for teachers or therapists).
- A minimum of one special field is also permitted.
- Integrated education is part of the curriculum.
- Students have a wide choice of different optional subjects.
- Only part of the sequence of subjects is regulated.
- The former area of the education of mentally handicapped children is divided into education for the learning disabled (a new term in Hungary) and education for the mentally handicapped.
- The period of long-term practice has been increased.
- Since the 1993–94 school year there has been an opportunity to work in graduate-level programmes at one of the largest universities in Budapest, the Eötvös Loránd

University, with the undergraduate degree from our College. This programme must be completed within two years (four semesters).

ACCEPTANCE OF THE REVISED PROGRAMME

The intentions of the college staff concerning the revision of the teacher education programme have raised discussion in professional journals and at meetings with teachers working in special schools. The most widely discussed topics are the following.

Initially there was resistance to the introduction of integration. Arguments referred to the lack of conditions and facilities in ordinary schools, the absence of support services, the rigid school programmes, and insufficient individualized teaching methods. Special teachers were mostly convinced that the best conditions could only be provided in special schools. There is still a fear of losing their pupils and that schools will be closed if integration is introduced and becomes better known and more popular among parents. With the increasing trend towards decentralization, education authorities might take over the responsibility of meeting special educational needs without providing the necessary financial resources. The new educational law hints at the possibility of free choice of schools, but there is a certain restriction in the case of disabled children and the financial conditions have not yet been regulated.

There also exists a fear that there will not be enough special teachers in special schools if teacher training offers other possibilities besides classroom teaching.

The notion of extending the number of children recognized as having special educational needs is not popular; the term 'special educational needs' does not officially exist. Mostly, medical criteria have been used for defining disabled children: their number is around 2.6 to 2.8 per cent of the whole population of similar age. Psychological functional disturbances and/or social deprivation do not apply to the official group of children with special needs. This means that children with different learning problems in the ordinary schools do not get the special support they require. The ordinary teachers do not possess the extra knowledge required for dealing with these pupils. The children often repeat classes and the number of drop-outs is quite high. According to the special teachers, working with children in ordinary schools is not part of their responsibility.

It is difficult to introduce new organizational ways of teaching, to change old and existing habits of teaching the whole class and not paying enough attention to individual problems. This is true both for ordinary and special schools.

FUTURE PLANS

The leadership of the College aims to change the College into a university and to provide the graduating students with a master's degree and later with the title of PhD. Contacts have to be built up with other teacher training colleges in two ways. First, there is a great need to provide our students with more theoretical and practical knowledge of so-called 'normal' education. We particularly intend to intensify this area as we are aware that the participants in our initial curriculum and training come to our College directly after finishing secondary school, without any preparation for or experience of the education of 'normal' children.

Secondly, we intend to plan and implement strategies with the aim of enriching the curricula in ordinary teacher training colleges with expertise in special educational needs and integration. This topic is lacking in most of the colleges or is only an optional subject. We think this will be quite possible in the future. Already we have made an important step in this direction by organizing two seminars on the UNESCO 'Schools for All' project, with Mel Ainscow of Cambridge University Institute of Education as workshop leader. We invited interested staff members from all Hungarian teacher education colleges and from some universities, as well as special teachers and classroom teachers from regular schools. The result was a very active and interested group of teacher trainers and teachers from different colleges, schools and pre-schools. This group was aware of the necessity for cooperation and of the fact that the existing walls between regular and remedial education can be broken down. Everybody agreed to work in a new way, and this group will continue to meet and exchange experiences. The members of the group want to work in close connection with the revision of the educational content of our College programme. We are also ready to coordinate this project in the future with our Hungarian TEMPUS partner, the Budapest Teacher Training College. The first step has been to have a common inclusive practice school. This step has been taken, and the school opened in September 1994. It is our hope that this school can serve as a model for future inclusive schooling. The new curricula of both colleges concerned with alternative ways for providing support for children with special needs may also serve as good models.

We believe that this practical work will be an efficient way to introduce new deas and approaches and to demonstrate concrete solutions adapted to the Hungarian educational system.

FURTHER READING

Csányi, Y. (1994) 'Neue Bestrebungen in der Ausbildung von Sonderpädagogen in Ungern.' In Ch. Amrein (ed.) *Die Sonderpädagogik im Prozess der Europäischen Integration* (Quarterly Journal for Health Education and its Related Fields, **63**, 2). Freiburg, Switzerland.
Hungarian Ministry of Culture and Education (1993) *Statistics on Special Education*. Budapest.

Chapter 15

Preparing Specialists to Work with Special Needs Children in Poland and at the Maria Grzegorzewska College for Special Education

Stefan Przybylski

INTRODUCTORY REMARKS

The social, political and economic events witnessed by Poland cannot be without influence on educational ideas and the state of the art in education. The nature of these changes provides both hope for a better future and a threat.

The Polish school system up to the end of 1990 was highly centralized. Curricula for schools at all levels were provided by the Ministry of National Education and were obligatory throughout the country. The new law on the education system approved by Parliament in September 1991 and a Higher Education Act of 1990 introduced a number of changes. The 1990 Act gave considerable autonomy to the universities with respect to the establishment of regulations governing their structure and organization. The Ministry of National Education oversees the use of those university funds allocated from the state budget and monitors the legality of university activities. The larger universities are completely independent with regard to the framing of their statutes establishing the organization of the university, study regulations, curricula, admission requirements and so on. In smaller universities decisions about such matters require further confirmation by the Minister.

SPECIAL EDUCATION IN POLAND – NEW TRENDS

The political and economic changes in Poland in the 1990s have brought about changes in state social policy towards the disabled. Current trends in social, educational and employment policies are characterized by efforts to provide disabled people with opportunities equal to those of other members of society. One of the examples of such efforts is promoting the employment of disabled people in open settings; another is the tendency to educate children with special needs in ordinary schools. The transition from the system of educating some disabled persons to a system which is integrated in family environment, age groups and school is a steady trend in special education. At present in Poland there is a system of education that is partly integrated and partly segregated.

Among the changes that can be observed we should stress the interest in disabled children who previously have not been included in the system of special education: children, for example, with cerebral palsy, autistic children, children with multiple handicaps and children who are profoundly mentally handicapped. Another new tendency is interest not only in those who are disabled but also in those who are in danger of becoming disabled. Special education is now perceived as covering the whole period from early childhood to old age. Also, more and more institutions for disabled people are being established by non-governmental institutions and organizations.

One characteristic feature of Poland's special education today is a trend towards socialization. Problems which for decades were the sole concern of the state have recently been taken up by social organizations, religious associations and private individuals. A good example of this phenomenon is the activity of parents having children with various handicaps who, desperately dissatisfied with the lack of concrete activity on the part of the state institutions, organized into strong pressure groups and, with the assistance of specialists, support the development of disabled children. The mass media are also devoting more time to these issues.

TEACHER TRAINING

The broad range of therapeutic and educational developments and the importance of their impact on people with special needs deriving from various kinds and degrees of impairment have led to a growing demand for trained specialists. Highly qualified teachers are needed, not only for special schools but also to work with students in the work environment, in the local environment or in institutions organizing recreation or leisure activities. That is why the task facing institutions training special teachers is becoming more and more important.

The concept of training specialists to work with disabled people in teacher training schools is based on a model of the five essential characteristics which a special teacher must have:

- a broad knowledge in such fields as psychology, pedagogy, sociology and other related disciplines;
- extensive knowledge of disturbed development as opposed to normal development;
- mastery of the methods of work at all ages and levels of development of disabled persons;
- a creative approach to all tasks undertaken in work with disabled people;
- an active attitude in influencing others in the environment who can cooperate in the rehabilitation and integration of disabled people.

Specialists to work with disabled people are trained in the pedagogical universities or at colleges of education. Full university studies with courses lasting five years are completed by means of a master's thesis written in accordance with scientific requirements, the successful graduate receiving the title of Master of Arts. Apart from universities, there are colleges with three-year courses leading to a professional degree with the title of 'bachelor'.

Among ten universities and pedagogical universities training special teachers, the Maria Grzegorzewska College for Special Education plays a leading role and trains specialists to work with all kinds of disabled persons. Half of Poland's special teachers have been trained at this college. Currently, the College trains teachers, educators and other specialists to work with children and young people who have impairments and/or problems in emotional and social adjustment.

In Polish educational administration, there is still a division of handicapped children by category of disability. Students of the Maria Grzegorzewska College can choose from among the following specializations: education of the mentally retarded; education of the deaf and hearing impaired; education of the blind and visually impaired; education of the chronically ill; speech therapy; prevention of social maladjustment and social work for the handicapped and their families.

In the light of the present state of special education for the disabled in Poland and of the prospects for its development, the college implements a model of training covering all the basic forms for the training of specialists to work with children and young people with special needs. These are:

- five-year full-time courses in special education;
- three-year full-time and extra-mural courses, for social workers who will work with handicapped children, in the prevention of social maladjustment and in the education of socially maladjusted children.
- three-semester postgraduate studies for those teachers who at present work with special needs children and who have graduated from faculties other than special education;
- a two-semester postgraduate programme for university graduates with a diploma in special education who wish to upgrade their qualifications. These studies update their knowledge in the field of special education.

It should be mentioned here that the five- and three-year full-time courses are for pupils from secondary schools who most often have had no teaching experience in the school environment. All students who study for five years are first prepared to work with normally developing children. After passing some examinations and some practice at ordinary schools, they learn to work with special needs children. All students who graduate from the five-year course are also qualified to work in primary schools. The curriculum of this programme includes courses in:

- biological and medical sciences (for example elements of anatomy and physiology, ecology, a basic knowledge of children's diseases, child psychiatry);
- social sciences (methodology, elements of philosophy and ethics, sociology and social policy, law as related to problems of human and child rights, etc.);
- general and clinical psychology;
- courses in education and specialized courses in given areas of special education.

During their studies the students undertake a number of training practice sessions, the fundamental purpose of which is to enable them to get acquainted with pupils, to develop working methods and to confront theoretical knowledge with school reality.

TRENDS IN SPECIAL TEACHER TRAINING

In the training which is carried out at the Maria Grzegorzewska College, a number of trends towards change can be observed. The range of programmes has increased, being no longer limited to the training of personnel to teach specific categories of disabled children. A gradual transition is taking place from a one-stage five-year programme to a two-stage one made up of two years plus three years. The availability of training for teachers from regular schools who have disabled students in their classes has been extended. Finally, there is a growing interest in teacher training for work with gifted children.

Looking at more general trends, we find that the political, economic and social transformations in Poland that have been under way for several years now have affected all areas of life, including the training of teachers for special education. The uniform teacher training system, based on five-year graduate studies, has recently been supplemented by three-year certification programmes. Despite the Ministry of National Education's strong support for the development and implementation of the three-year programmes, higher education establishments have not given up the five-year graduate studies; they are carrying both forms of training. Moreover, in the area of special education five-year studies are very popular among students, because graduates have the qualifications to work not only with disabled children but also in mainstream schools.

New programmes are being developed in areas where there have been no highly qualified specialists, for example the training of social workers to work with disabled adults; the training of kindergarten and elementary school teachers for work with disabled children attending integrated schools or classes, which comprise a total of 15 to 20 pupils including three to five disabled children; training teachers for multi-handicapped children and so on. These specialists are usually trained in the postgraduate programmes, in the in-service training courses and/or by means of three-year extra-mural studies.

It should be noted finally that the training of special teachers is being organized not only by state institutes and universities, but also by private individuals, foundations and associations. However, the quality of this training does not meet the recognized standards, primarily owing to a lack of adequately qualified teacher trainers.

Chapter 16

Teacher Education for Special Needs in Spain

Angeles Parrilla Latas

INTRODUCTION

Teacher education in Spain is currently undergoing important changes due to the reform of the education system. This chapter is concerned with the degree courses, ideas, training structure and general contents of the new curricula in the field of special education, foreseen in the new educational system.

The chapter is divided into three parts. First I will explain some ideas about the sociopolitical context, theoretical bases and organizational structure of the new Spanish education system, and the role of special education within this system. In the second part I will move on to describe the teacher education centres in Spain, along with their goals and objectives, their course contents, and the professionals to whom the courses apply. Finally, I will reflect upon the current difficulties and dilemmas found in the training of teachers for special education and yet to be resolved.

SPECIAL EDUCATION IN THE SPANISH EDUCATIONAL SYSTEM

We could begin by characterizing the idea of special education, as conceived in the new reforms, as being coherent with the integration which has been under continual development in Spain since 1985. Current education policy envisages special education as forming part of the general educational system, rather than as an entirely separate structure; it is the role of the general educational system to offer the appropriate conditions and resources to meet the special educational needs of students.

The key idea is that Spain is a democracy with a parliamentary monarchy. We have a democratic central government and 17 autonomous communities, each with its own self-government (home rule). This means that we have a common juridical basis for all Spanish citizens and variability within the autonomies. For example, emerging from the central state we have a common structure for the educational system and a common curriculum, but there are wide divergencies of practice between the autonomous communities.

Educational integration is a right in Spain, but some communities have full-school integration while in others it is only partial. Some communities therefore have special schools and services as well as integration while others only have regular schools and services.

The background to this situation is to be found in the 1978 Spanish Constitution, which specifies that every citizen has the right to a public education regardless of his or her race, ethnic origin, religion, gender, intellectual capacity and so on. But it is since the Educational Integration Law of 1985 that special education has been faced with the most important changes. This law introduced a progressive experimental programme lasting eight years. This means that schools implemented integration in a progressive way, starting with infant education in the first year and increasing the experience by one level every year. Furthermore, the integration programme allowed schools to partici-pate on a voluntary basis; each individual school has had the choice whether or not to undertake the programme during this eight-year period. In fact at this moment not all the primary schools in Spain are developing integration. In spite of this, integration in secondary education has been undertaken as a continuation of the initial integration programme, again as a voluntary option for schools.

Two ideas, *diversity* and *comprehensivity*, are fundamental when it comes to out-lining and understanding how this educational policy is being developed (MEC, 1989a).

Diversity refers to the recognition and acceptance of the fact that education must respond to the needs of all students, something which has led, for the first time in Spain, to a common educational policy for all. Every student enjoys free access to any state educational institution. Diversity is as much a means of organization as it is an objective.

The idea of *comprehensivity* means the pursuit of a single, common curriculum for all. The comprehensive school system is based on the belief in the enhancement of the common core contents and experiences of compulsory school-age students, with teaching carried out in common institutions and regular classrooms, regardless of the personal situation of the students.

In this way, all schools (state-run and private) must follow a common basic curricu-lum design with a prescriptive base which is adapted at the various levels of the state, the autonomous community, and the locality. The last step in this chain is taken by each particular school which adapts the curriculum offered by its autonomous community to the needs of the institution as a whole, of each scholastic level, of classes and of individual students.

These curricular and organizational ideas may be easily identified within the integra-tion policy begun in 1985. Despite this, the new law (MEC, 1990) for the organization of the educational system, which is gradually being introduced, continues to support separate special schools working alongside, and apart from, general schools, in clear contradiction to the foregoing ideas.

In general, education is compulsory from the age of 6 until 16, with the system divided into three stages, each with its own type of school:

Infant or pre-school education (0–6 years): teaching is carried out in two separate stages, the first from 0 to 3 years and the second from 3 to 6 years. This level of schooling is not compulsory.

Primary education (6–12 years): teaching is carried out in three separate stages, from 6 to 8 years, from 8 to 10 years and from 10 to 12 years. This level of schooling is compulsory.

Secondary education (12–18 years): teaching is carried out in two stages, the first compulsory stage from 12 to 16 years, and the second optional stage from 16 to 18 years. The latter is divided into two distinct courses: *bachillerato* (preparation for university studies) and *formación professional* (practical training in various fields, normally leading to employment).

TRAINING FOR SPECIAL EDUCATION

Initial training for special education

All the initial training courses are undertaken at university level. The education of infant and primary teachers (in any specialization) and training in social education and speech therapy, as well as the degree in psychopedagogy, take place at university. However, training leads to different levels of university qualification (diploma level and full degree) in the different professional courses. This is because the Spanish university system is three-tiered, with a first cycle (three years) leading to a diploma, a second cycle (two years) leading to a full degree (*licenciatura*) and a final cycle (2 to 5 years) leading to a doctorate (*doctorado*).

University training faculties: diploma level

Infant and primary school teachers, social educators and speech therapists are trained in these institutions. The qualification is at diploma level, which corresponds to the first cycle of Spanish university studies.

A chief characteristic of the structure of initial training in these centres is the dual-training model. The two main qualifications to which the courses lead are: 'teacher specialized in general teaching' (by subject and level) and 'teacher specialized in special education'.

This raises a controversial issue, which has been debated in other countries with more experience in integration policy, as well as in Spain itself. The problem arises in organizing and structuring comprehensive, integrated schools and classes with teachers trained only in general education. Such teachers will have studied only one topic in special educational needs.

A second characteristic is that special teacher training is conceived as a specialization, not as a requirement for all teachers in general education. The special teacher trainee may obtain one of two qualifications: 'teacher specialized in special education' or 'teacher specialized in hearing and language'. These two qualifications are directed at training support teachers and withdrawal teachers in the new nursery and primary schools.

Thirdly, specialization is developed in initial training, without links with practice and with no direct contact with general teaching. That is, the trainee becomes a special teacher as a result of specialized initial university training which is theoretical. There is no requirement to have first been a general teacher with some experience in general education. Two important outcomes of this model of training can be perceived:

- There is a weakness in the links between theory and practice. Specialization is possible solely on the basis of academic, theoretical knowledge.
- There is the risk of problems in the relationship between general and specialized teachers. With the model of specialization as part of initial training, it is possible that a special teacher who has never worked in general education may try to assist a general teacher with the curricular problems of integration in general teaching. Problems of credibility, expertise and so on can easily arise and block the necessary cooperative relations between the general and the special teacher.

As a fourth point, we may indicate the problems associated with the orientation of the course content of teacher training. Proposed plans approved by the Spanish Ministry of Education may be regarded as 'categorical', in that the various categories of disability have served as the focus for the structuring of the contents of the two new courses. Moreover, too much emphasis has been laid upon the medical and clinical aspects of teaching children with disabilities. A quick glance at the titles of special education courses will confirm this 'categorical' orientation. (The numbers in brackets refer to credits, each credit representing, as a norm, ten hours of lectures.)

Teacher specialized in special education: core units of the speciality.

Didactic and Organizational Aspects of Special Education (6)
Evolutionary and Educational Aspects of Impaired Hearing (6)
Evolutionary and Educational Aspects of Mental Handicap (9)
Evolutionary and Educational Aspects of Physical Handicap (6)
Evolutionary and Educational Aspects of Visual Handicap (6)
Physical Education of Students with Special Educational Needs (4)
Craft and Musical Expression (4)
Behavioural and Personality Disorders (6)
Educational Treatment of Written Language Disabilities (9)
Practicum (32)

Teacher specialized in hearing and language: core units of the speciality

Anatomy, Physiology and Neurology of Language (4)
Evolutionary Aspects of Thought and Language (4)
Development of Linguistic Ability (8)
Linguistics (8)
Psychopathology of Hearing and Language (8)
Alternative Systems of Communication (4)
Educational Treatment of Hearing and Language Disabilities (8)
Educational Treatment of Oral and Written Disabilities (8)
Practicum (32)

Other special education training diplomas are offered to speech therapists and social workers. Professionals with these qualifications are not teachers: they are special education professionals who work within the school system, but do not teach.

The first of these specialized courses is the speech therapy speciality. This training course aims to give basic theoretical and practical knowledge to develop prevention, assessment and intervention activities concerned with language disabilities in adults and infants. The basic course content, like the 'hearing and language teacher' course is more concerned with medical and clinical explanation than educative intervention.

Diploma in speech therapy (logopedia): core units of the speciality

Anatomy and Physiology of the Organs of Language and Hearing (8)
Exploration of Language, Speech and Voice Disabilities (6)
Linguistic Intervention in Language Difficulties (8)
Linguistic Intervention in Speech and Voice Disabilities (8)
General and Applied Linguistics (6)
General and Language Neurology (8)
Pathology of Hearing and Language (8)
Psychology of Language Acquisition and Development (8)
Specific Intervention Techniques in Language (12)
Practicum (32)

Finally, the social educator diploma is for a professional who works in the field of non-formal education, in the integration of socially maladjusted young people, and in socio-educative intervention. Social educators work with social organizations which have educational but not academic aims. For example, they work in social organizations aimed at leisure activities, sports and cultural events, or in residential centres, adult centres and so on and deal with a wide range of ages.

Diploma in social education: core units of the speciality

General Didactics (8)
Permanent Education (6)
Educative Intervention in Social Maladjustment (9)
New Technology in Education (4)
Leadership of Children in Social or Cultural Situations (6)
Developmental Psychology (9)
Social and Organizational Psychology (6)
Social Anthropology and Sociology (6)
Contemporary Education Theories and Institutions (4)

University training faculties: degree level

Degree-level (five-year course) training in special education has, until now, led to another common degree in Spain. The most specific course at this level, before the present reform of programmes of study, was entitled 'Therapeutic Pedagogy', and this could be obtained at university faculties in the second cycle (fourth and fifth years) of the general studies in pedagogy.

The new course in this area is named 'Psychopedagogy'. The full psychopedagogical professional degree can be obtained only after the primary or social education diploma or the first cycle of the psychology course (each one a three-year course). It is then a two-year (second-cycle) course in a university faculty. The basic goal of this course is to give a scientific knowledge of basic and applied aspects of individual and organizational academic and vocational assessment, of support in integration processes and of the treatment of learning problems. This kind of training is directed at professionals who usually work in assessment teams, in consulting projects at school or community level, teacher training, specialized intervention with pupils and so on.

Owing to the variability between universities in this kind of training I shall only present the general goals of the full degree course in psychopedagogy and the common subjects of this course nationwide. There is a compulsory curriculum in general subjects, while every university completes the course with its own subjects and specialization focus.

The following are the common and compulsory subjects that may be taken in each university with different specializations available as course options (assessment, support, etc.).

Degree in psychopedagogy: core units of the speciality

Assessment in Education (6)
Curriculum Design and Innovation (6)
Special Education (8)
Learning Disabilities and Psychopedagogical Intervention (6)
Psychopedagogical Intervention in Development Disorders (6)
Research Methodology in Education (6)
Assessment and Intervention Psychopedagogical Models (6)
Vocational Assessment (4)
Instructional Psychology (8)
Practicum (12)

As we can see, a general focus on special education is an element of this course: two subjects from eight are about special education ('Special Education' and 'Learning Disabilities and Psychopedagogical Intervention'). The training path that a student can adopt to arrive at this stage (from general to specialized teacher training, from first-cycle pedagogy studies to psychology and also from a social education diploma) draws a wide range of students with diverse backgrounds and training experiences; this probably explains the general orientation of the subject linked to special education in this course. As a result, it is not possible for us to analyse the trends and focus of this course, because it depends whether the individual university chooses to create more general, open and wider training, focusing on diversity in schools and students with special educational needs for every psychopedagogue, or alternatively to prefer more specific orientation in traditional training for a specialized psychopedagogue in special education.

In-service training for special education

In-service teacher training has two main general goals (MEC, 1989h) The first is to update teachers' knowledge and prepare them for the basic work of adapting the curricula to individual schools and students. Secondly, the new model of teacher training is directed to preparing teachers to work in new stages and areas of the school system.

In-service teacher training is organized from the Ministry point of view, within the framework of the following ideas (Prats, 1991):

- It is a professional, practice-based training programme, which stresses the links between theory and practice in such a way that theory guides the reflective thinking of teachers about their practice.
- It is school focused. This means that the whole school as a learning community, not the individual teacher, is the basic unit for training. This training has to answer to collegiate needs and processes in school because collaborative training and reflection are assumed to be the key to professional and organizational development.
- It uses a diversity of strategies and a number of organizational models which respond to the specific and particular nature of the different training needs.
- It enhances decentralization. Every autonomous community has its own in-service teacher training plan, and every teacher training centre has a local plan based on locally identified training needs. Finally, every school has to make decisions and participate in its own training process.

This is the reason why there is no specific state programme for special education teacher training. Each autonomous community develops its own training programme in the special education field in order to answer to the needs and sensibilities specific to that community.

Teachers' centres are the basic institutions for in-service education, but training requirements are also fulfilled by the educational science institutes (for secondary teachers); advisory teachers (in different areas or at different levels); and various kinds of collaboration with university departments, research institutes, companies, local administrations and teachers' associations.

In-service teacher training in special education has three functions:

- *Specialization*, directed at general teachers. This training takes the form of postgraduate study courses of one to two years' duration. Autonomous communities and universities under contract are the training agents.
- Updating the *resources and knowledge* of regular teachers. This is the improvement of knowledge about special educational needs, curricular modifications and other professional activities linked to the integration process.
- *Focusing and development*. This provides an even greater degree of specialization for special education teachers, or for special education degree holders (advisory teachers, multiprofessional teams, psychologists and psychopedagogues).

These are the general and policy trends. An analysis of their practical implications can be obtained from the research of Balbás (1993), which focuses specifically on the in-service training needs of general teachers in the area of special needs, and which also analyses the point of view and the participation of teachers in special needs in-service educational programmes. Parrilla and Balbás (1995) and Balbás and Parrilla (1995) are two works aimed at analysing the conceptual and practical problems and issues linked to initial and in-service teacher education in Spain in the area of special educational needs.

SOME OUTSTANDING PROBLEMS AND DILEMMAS OF TEACHER TRAINING FOR SPECIAL EDUCATION

An issue for both initial and in-service teacher education is the need to rethink and redefine the conceptual basis of courses in special education. A general orientation to integration and inclusive education is the approach agreed to be appropriate to the Integration Law, and the ideas I have put forward about the need for diversity and about the comprehensive school are essential to the educational reform. It is not possible to assume conceptual ideas linked to a positive value of human diversity and a point of view which understands that there is a continuum of differences between people, thus justifying a comprehensive curriculum and a school for all, and then to organize teacher training which enhances and categorizes the kinds of diversity, maintains a division between special and general professionals and carries on with a double way of training. The messages that the teachers and educators are receiving from the legislation and the training are in clear contradiction and seem to imply a wrong way of implementing integration in the schools.

Whatever this conceptual point of view, training can also be analysed within other parameters, such as content trends. As we saw when we analysed the subject matter of initial teacher-training courses in special education, the focus was on a categorical orientation about the nature and kinds of special needs. However, since teacher education aims at preparation for work at school level the student teachers need more than casual and explanatory knowledge, they need practical and didactic knowledge which allows them to address questions of curricular design and development in integrated settings. In spite of this, categorical knowledge about defects is the legal option chosen in the content orientation courses. Categorical orientation assumes a linear and casual relation between categories of defect and the behaviour and learning of students, whatever the category. It corresponds to a kind of technological knowledge more oriented towards clinical than towards educational, curricular and organizational explanation and intervention. In opposition to this, research and practice in the training needs of teachers have found that, because of the individual variability between pupils and classes, the kind of knowledge that a teacher needs in order to work with a focus on diversity is not causal and normative about either students or intervention; rather it is descriptive and explicative in the sense that enhances enquiry-oriented practice and teaching (Blackhurst, 1981, 1982; Blackhurst *et al.*, 1987; Reynolds and Lakin, 1987; Balbás, 1993). This means taking into account the importance in the education of teachers of the growth of knowledge in action as well as reflective and exploratory teaching, as significant ways to work with the variability that diversity in schools implies. This kind of knowledge is particularly significant since course-content orientation in teacher education may largely determine the development of an open, inductive learning and attitude to the practice of integration, or the opposite.

The character of initial training in the special education course for primary teachers involves another misconceived orientation. Several studies and reviews (Balbás, 1993; Pugach, 1986, 1987; Reynolds and Lakin, 1987) have noted the risks and difficulties linked to this option of specialization in special education as part of initial teacher training: a strong separation between teachers, inadequate cooperation, a lack of concern on the part of the general teacher for the contribution and views of the special teacher, and the poor knowledge of general education that the special teacher has at the end of the teacher training period.

We need to consider too the initial and in-service specialization in special education leading to a university degree in psychopedagogy for those who will work in individual and organizational assessment within special education, in teacher training in special education at initial and in-service level, and in direct individual support to students with special education needs. New plans at this level look at special education within a narrow framework, as it is only an introductory foundation subject. The different training paths and backgrounds to be found among students highlight a weakness in the situation which needs to be analysed in every university in a uniform way. The time for this has now come.

The lack of a serious endeavour to include special education in the initial training of general primary teachers is another important problem, because these teachers will work in integrated classroom settings. The two separate training courses (general and special), and the study of only a general subject for the general teachers in initial training seems a poor answer to the challenge of working with diversity in classrooms. A polyvalent, 'cross-categorical' framework would be an appropriate way to begin to address these issues.

Equally important is the in-service training of current general teachers working in integrated classrooms. Because they do not have this, technical, attitudinal, personal and social problems arise and threaten to undermine the integration process. The development of the policy guidelines that we have outlined needs to start only – as Balbás (1993) has pointed out – after the study of the teacher training needs of integration. Obviously, this can be an important and successful way of offering appropriate and relevant study courses to teachers. Furthermore, we need to move away from a policy which implements a programme of integration and educational reform without undertaking in-service training of all the teachers: at present it is a voluntary and personal decision on the part of every general teacher whether or not to engage in an in-service training course. We need to consider making in-service training of all teachers compulsory.

Finally the above review of courses reveals the lack of provision of education in special needs for secondary school teachers. These teachers do not have pedagogical or didactical knowledge in their initial training, which is always subject or area oriented. Only in the Course of Pedagogical Capacity, developed in the institutes of educational sciences – which is a compulsory, part-time one-year course for these teachers before access to practical teaching can be undertaken – is there a need to include knowledge of how to diversify in teaching objectives and methods. Furthermore, teachers' centres need to develop a similar trend in planning and offering in-service courses which include diversity as a topic in every subject and course. The development of this activity will be essential if we are to safeguard the continuity of the primary integration process and to offer to each student access to an adult life in employment or higher education.

There are undoubtedly many problems, but we expect that a significant number will be overcome as we develop teacher training which combines the ideological and policy assumptions about diversity and schools with a 'cross-categorical' content orientation, a common structure and organization for general and special teachers and professionals, a coherent policy for the in-service training of general teachers, as well obviously as an extension of the training to secondary teachers if we want to extend integration to secondary schools.

REFERENCES

Balbás, M.J. (1993) 'Las necesidades formativas del profesor tutor de EGB ante la integración: Evaluación diagnóstica y propuesta de formación'. Unpublished doctoral thesis, University of Seville.
Balbás, M.J. and Parrilla, A. (1995) 'Tendencias en la formación del profesorado de cara a la integración (II): formación permanente'. *Revista de Educación Especial* (in press).
Blackhurst, A.E. (1981) 'Non-categorical teacher preparation: problems and promises'. *Exceptional Children*, **48**, 197–205.
Blackhurst, A.E. (1982) 'Non-categorical special education teacher preparation'. In M. Reynolds (ed.) *The Future of Mainstreaming: Next Steps in Teacher Education*. Reston, VA: Council for Exceptional Children.
Blackhurst, A.E., Bott, D. and Cross, P. (1987) 'Non-categorical special education personnel preparation'. In M. Wang, M. Reynolds and H. Walberg (eds) *Handbook of Special Education: Research and Practice, Vol. I*. Oxford: Pergamon Press.
MEC (Ministerio de Educación y Ciencia) (1989a) *Libro Blanco para la Reforma del Sistema Educativo*. Madrid: MEC.
MEC (Ministerio de Educación y Ciencia) (1989b) *Plan de Investigación Educativa y de Formación de Profesorado*. Madrid, MEC.
MEC (Ministerio de Educación y Ciencia) (1990) *Ley Orgánica de Ordenación del Sistema Educativo*. Madrid: MEC.
Parrilla, A. and Balbás, M.J. (1995) 'Tendencias en la formación del profesorado de cara a la integración (I): formación inicial'. *Revista de Educación Especial* (in press).
Prats, J. (1991) 'Los centros de profesores y los asesores de formación permanente del profesorado: elementos para la construcción de un modelo'. *Bordon*, **43**(2), 163–7.
Pugach, M. (1986) 'The national education reports and special education: implications for teacher preparation'. *Exceptional Children*, **53**(4), 308–14.
Pugach, M. (1987) 'Special education categories as constraints on the reform of the teacher education'. Paper presented at the American Educational Research Association conference, San Francisco.
Reynolds, M. and Lakin, C (1987) 'Noncategorical special education: models for research and practice'. In M. Wang, M. Reynolds and H. Walberg (eds) *Handbook of Special Education: Research and Practice Vol. I*. Oxford: Pergamon Press.

FURTHER READING

Balbás, M.J. (1991) 'Una aproximación a las necesidades formativas de todos los profesores ante la diversidad'. In M. Zabalza and J.R. Alberte (eds) *Educación Especial y Formación de Profesores*. Santiago: Torculo.
LISMI (1982) Ley (Law) 13/1982 de 7 de Abril de Integración Social de los Minusválidos. *Boletin Oficial del Estado* (*BOE*) 30 April.

Muntaner, J.J. (1992) 'La formación del profesorado como elemento dinamizador de la integración y la reforma'. Paper presented at the IX Jornadas de Universidades y Educación Especial, Madrid.

Parrilla, A. (1992) *El Profesor ante la Integración Escolar: Investigación y Formación*. Madrid: Cincel.

Parrilla, A. (1992) *La Integración Escolar como Experiencia Institucional*. Seville: GID.

Real Decreto 334/1985 de 6 de Marzo, de Ordenación de la Educación Especial. *Boletin Oficial del Estado (BOE)*, 16 March.

Vázquez Ruiz, C. (1992) 'La formación del profesorado de enseñanza secundaria en lo que respecta a la atención de los alumnos/as con necesidades educativas especiales'. In M.A. Zabalza and J.R. Alberte (eds) *Educación Especial y Formación de Profesores*. Santiago: Torculo.

Zabalza, M.A. and Alberte, J.R. (eds) (1992) *Educación Especial y Formación de Profesores*. Santiago: Tórculo.

Zabalza, M.A. (1993) 'Formación de profesorado y educación especial'. Paper presented at the X Jornadas de Universidades y Educación Especial, Santiago, June.

Chapter 17

The Training of Special Educators in Sweden

Jerry Rosenqvist and Ingvar Sandling

INTRODUCTION

Special education in Sweden has a history and a future and so has the training of special educators.

Sweden has a surface area of 449, 964 square kilometres and (in 1990) a population of 8,527,036 million (*Statistisk Årsbók*, 1991). The average population density is 21 inhabitants per square kilometre with the most dense areas in the southern part. From north to south the distance is 1530 km and from east to west around 450 kilometres. About 15 per cent of the land area is situated north of the polar circle. The nation is divided into 25 counties, which in most cases also form municipality clusters, so-called county councils, with responsibility for regular health care and medical attendance and, until 1995, schools for mentally disabled pupils. There are 144 municipalities with responsibility for the provision of regular comprehensive education; after 1995 this will include the education of mentally disabled pupils.

School is compulsory in Sweden from the age of 7 to 16. Since the school year 1993–94 parents have been entitled to send their children to school at the age of 6, but so far very few parents have made that choice. Before the age of 7 children may attend day nursery or, at the age of 6, a pre-school in which the municipality is required to offer them a place. Although upper secondary school is not compulsory it is completed by more than 90 per cent of the age cohort.

The compulsory comprehensive school (*grundskola*) comprises grades 1–9. There is an increasing number of private schools in Sweden but so far under 2 per cent of the relevant population are attending these schools. The non-compulsory upper secondary school which is known as the gymnasium comprises three or four years of education. The vocational education forms have an extended practicum.

All education in Sweden is free of charge. Pupils get free books, a free school meal per day and, when needed, free transportation to and from school until upper secondary level. Parents get a child allowance until the child is 16 years old and thereafter, if the child still attends school, a prolonged allowance until the age of 19.

The funding of schools at comprehensive and upper secondary level is shared by the state and the municipality, with the latter bearing the main part of the costs. Until recently the state shared the burden equally with the municipality and at this time the resources for special education were more or less earmarked. Today the municipality gets a grant of money for many public services, among them education, which it is free to use in what it considers the most appropriate way.

Special schools, which are run by the state, are now very rare in Sweden. In 1989, 639 pupils attended such schools for hearing- and/or speech-impaired or deaf pupils. Only 45 students attended special schools for the blind. In addition 11,421 pupils were registered as mentally disabled (1990) but more than 95 per cent of these attended regular schools, although in classrooms of their own; 1008 of these pupils were individually integrated in ordinary classrooms (*Statistiska Meddelanden*, 1991). Mobility-impaired pupils as well as most of the blind and visually impaired pupils attend ordinary classes in regular school. So does the vast majority of pupils with other special needs.

THE GENERAL SCHOOL SYSTEM

History and background

In 1842 Sweden got its first common school law, 'The People's School Statute' to provide a national system of elementary education. This established the state primary school, *folkskola*, which functioned in parallel with the cathedral schools, which were reserved for the children of wealthy people, but it was not fully developed until around 1880. In 1878 the primary school got its first curriculum, the 'normal plan', and in 1882 this form of school was divided into a two-year 'small school' followed by a four-year 'big school'. In 1894 the dualistic, elementary part of the school was abandoned and a three-year 'lower school' for all was adopted.

In 1919 Sweden got its first national curriculum in a modern sense. In 1936 the elementary school was extended to seven years. Transition to the non-compulsory secondary school could take place after either grade 4 or grade 6 of the elementary school. It could be completed after five or four years respectively with a 'real-examen', or the student could apply for entry to the upper secondary school (gymnasium) after four or three years respectively. Thus a 'maturity exam' could be completed after 4 + 4 + 4 or 6 + 3 + 4 years (Egidius, 1978; Rust, 1988).

The present situation

In 1962 the Swedish Parliament passed the nine-year comprehensive Grundskolere-form. The *grundskola* is divided into three forms (junior, middle and senior level) with three years spent in each. It may be followed by upper secondary school for three or four years.

Upper limits for class size are no longer set in the compulsory school, but most schools try to adhere to an earlier recommendation, which was a maximum of 25 at the junior level and a maximum of 30 thereafter.

A new curriculum (Lpo 94, 1994) for the compulsory school, including special schools, effective from 1 July 1995, was passed by Parliament in March 1994. In the introduction it is strongly stressed that:

- all children should be entitled to an education of equal value regardless of where in the nation they attend school;
- consideration should be given to the individual student's requirements;
- some of the goals should be reached by most students, whereas some goals arc only to be aimed at.

These statements might at first glance appear to be very general, but the intention is to indicate strongly that our compulsory school must be *a school for all children*.

THE SPECIAL EDUCATION SYSTEM

History and background

Three main periods may be discerned in the history of special education in Sweden: the stage of non-differentiation; the stage of differentiation; and the stage of integration.

The first stage lasted until the turn of the century, or, to be more realistic about the number of pupils concerned, until around 1950. All children were allowed to attend school and those who failed either had to leave school or remain a second year in a class. There were many disabled children who never gained access to school.

The beginnings of the second stage go back a long way; however it encompassed only those children with manifest impairments. The first attempt to initiate formal education for disabled children was made in 1809, when Mr Pär Aron Borg started an Institute for Blind and Deaf Children in Stockholm. It was not until 1879 that blind and deaf children were separated into two different schools. In 1866 Miss Emanuella Carlbeck started teaching a group of mentally retarded children in Gothenburg. She is considered the real pioneer in that field in Sweden. In 1870 the government decided to give financial support to her 'Idiot School' as well as to a similar school in Stockholm (Blomberg, 1934). At the turn of the century a few special institutions, with schools, were started for mobility-impaired children.

It is obvious that, for many years, only a small number of disabled children had the opportunity to attend special schools. Schools for deaf children were made compulsory in 1889 and those for the blind in 1896. As far as the mentally retarded are concerned, they were not covered by any regulations until 1944, when a law made schools for the educable mentally retarded (EMR) compulsory. The 1967 Care Law gave all mentally disabled children the right to education: it was no longer necessary to be 'educable'. On the contrary, the school had to adjust to all children and provide them with suitable instruction.

In the regular schools there were, of course, many children who had learning difficulties of different kinds. A first move in segregating such pupils was made in 1879 when the city of Norrköping established so-called help classes. In 1940 there were about 300 help classes with about 4000 pupils all over the country, and in 1952 the figures had increased to 856 classes with 11,500 pupils. Until the latter part of the 1950s placement in special schools or in special classes was the most common solution to problems of special needs education and the differentiation is obvious.

In the following decade the system of special education was established, comprising special classes for 'school-immaturity', 'observation' (behavioral disorders), reading/writing difficulties and visual/hearing impairments. The number of special classes within the regular schools increased from 2.3 per cent in 1945 to 9.1 per cent in 1968. From then on there was a gradual decrease and by 1977 the figure had fallen to around 3.5 per cent.

Besides special classes the schools could arrange 'particular special education' (*särskild specialundervisning*) in so-called clinics, where pupils could get extra support individually or in small groups for some hours a week. It was gradually understood that this constant increase in the percentage of pupils enrolled in special education was unjust and even threatening. Hence, in 1971 the school authorities fixed the special education allocation at 0.3 hours per week per pupil. It was now up to the local school boards to find the best solution for their school district; it was hoped that they would also adopt other models as well as special classes.

The third stage, which was a movement towards integration, signified an extension of this latter form of special education and a reduction in the number of special classes. The old concept of 'particular special education' was eventually changed to 'coordinated special education' (*samordnad specialundervisning*), which paved the way for special education to take place in the ordinary classroom with the support of a 'partner (special) teacher'.

The present situation

The aim of policy in special education has been to make it an integrated part of regular instruction. Special classes within the regular school do not formally exist. All extra support to children with special needs should be delivered either in the ordinary classroom or in smaller groups for a few hours a week. There are a couple of important exceptions, however. In many communities there are special day schools where children with severe behavioural disorders can stay even after school hours. As the local communities take over responsibility for the developmentally disabled, only mildly retarded (IQ 55–70) children will be placed in regular classes. The severely retarded will still remain in special classes. It is also possible to form groups for visually or hearing-impaired children, but as there are very few of these groups such provisions are available only in the largest communities.

Since 1990 no resources have been earmarked for special education. The result of this new freedom has been that services to special needs children are delivered in many different ways. In some school districts this has even resulted in the school choosing to have smaller classes with no extra resources for special education. It should also be added that while the removal of earmarked money has been an important force for change, the present situation also owes something to the economic cuts to which Swedish schools, like other parts of the public sector, have been subject. Signals from the new government indicate that there will be even less public money to spend for the rest of this century. As one result the number of special teachers has been reduced during the late 1980s, and this tendency seems likely to be even stronger in the very near future.

THE TRAINING OF REGULAR TEACHERS

History and background

In order to supply the schools with skilled teachers the school law of 1842 also required the cathedral cities to establish 'teacher seminars' including a one-year teacher training course. In 1880 this teacher education was extended to three years' study following on six years of primary school. Even with these very limited requirements it took many years to get the number of qualified teachers needed. In 1936 teacher education was reformed. 'Small school' teachers now had a three-year and 'big school' a four-year education after the 'real exam' (nine years' study); or alternatively, both groups could take a two-year training after the 'maturity exam' (twelve years' study). In order to adapt teacher education to the need of the *grundskola*, the old 'seminary' was gradually reformed during the 1960s to become the school of education or 'teachers' high school', which in 1977 became part of the university.

The present situation

The division of teacher education at compulsory school level was contrary to the intentions of the *grundskola* reform. To make it fit better with the idea of a unified *grundskola*, teacher education changed in 1988. Today we educate only two types of *grundskola* teachers, 'early teachers' and 'later teachers' (to date no more appropriate terminology has been found). Early teachers are eligible to work with grades 1 to 7 and later teachers with grades 4 to 9. There is thus an overlap for grades 4 to 7 which means that a change of teacher may take place at any time during this period.

All students get ten credits (a credit equals one week) in special education. These credits are normally not given in the form of a special course but integrated with the other subjects. Because of the reduced number of special teachers in the compulsory school there is a great need for ordinary teachers to have a good knowledge of special needs pupils. Special teachers are also getting a new role in the school, meaning that they will spend less time with individual children than in the past. Instead they will serve much more as consultants to regular teachers, school administrators and parents.

THE TRAINING OF SPECIAL EDUCATORS

History and background

The first special teachers had no formal training, but some of them studied and practised abroad for shorter or longer periods. In Sweden the training of special teachers started in a very informal way at the end of the last century. It was common for young girls to work as unpaid trainees at the special school for deaf and blind in Stockholm and at Miss Carlbeck's school for the mentally retarded. Each year teachers then chose one or two girls considered suitable, and gave them an in-service training that became more and more formal as the years went by. Very soon these schools became officially recognized as 'seminars' for the training of special teachers and received extra financial state support for that purpose. Such was the case in 1874 for the deaf and blind at 'Manillaskolan' in Stockholm and in 1879 for the mentally retarded at 'Slagsta skola' in Fittja (Blomberg, 1934). In 1955 the seminar for the mentally retarded was integrated with a regular seminar in Stockholm but it was not until 1977 that the training of teachers for the visually and hearing-impaired was undertaken by the Stockholm School of Education.

Special teachers in the regular schools have always started as regular teachers with a regular teacher training background. Special teacher education was thus a form of further training. The first teachers who attended such further training were the special class teachers. At first these courses had the character of seminars or shorter courses, but soon they became one-semester courses at a seminar in Stockholm. The education of special class teachers was more or less provisional from 1921 to 1961. The first centrally regulated training of special teachers, consisting of two-semester courses, started in 1962 at the Schools of Education in Stockholm and Gothenburg (Bladini, 1990). To begin with, these courses were multifold in order to cater for the needs of special teachers working in regular schools and in schools for mentally retarded pupils. During the 1970s the training was divided into three different lines:

1. A two-semester line for special teachers for:
    - children with slight developmental disability (IQ 55–70);
    - teaching a special class or remedial group;
    - teaching an observation class or remedial group;
    - instruction of children with reading/writing problems;
    - instruction of children with mobility impairments in a class or remedial group;
    - instruction of children with visual problems;
2. A three- or four-semester line for special teachers for:
    - children with severe visual problems;
    - children with severe hearing problems.
3. A two-semester education for special teachers (including pre-school) for:
    - children with speech problems;
    - children in hospitals;
    - the training school for developmentally disabled children (IQ below 55);
    - the activity and vocational training of developmentally disabled students.

Over the years the philosophy around special education has changed from definition of special problems and methods of dealing with them, to the following views expressed by SIA (1976, p. 278):

> Special education is no longer a different education aiming to adjust some, relatively few pupils. Its task is to deliberately test and develop common educational theories in the search for further support which may be needed by many pupils for longer or shorter periods, in their natural environment. Special education thus will become something that characterizes every day work for all staff at school.

The philosophy around the training of special teachers naturally changed as well, and in 1989 special teacher education was transformed into an 'additional line for special pedagogues' (SFS 745; 1990). The name is important because it indicates that it is no longer necessary to be a teacher to take this training. The entry regulation stated only that the applicant must 'have a basic teacher education or 100 credits [five semesters] in university studies and have worked for at least five years within school or in child care, or in other activities relevant to the training' (Malmö School of Education, 1990, p. 13).

The present situation

From 1989 to 1992 many different categories had the opportunity to enter a training programme for special pedagogues. It was considered by many a very positive reform that professionals such as psychologists, social workers, physiotherapists and occupational therapists could take this training. After having gone through the programme they were not teachers, but they had undoubtedly achieved deeper knowledge about special needs children, adolescents and adults.

In 1993 the government decided (SFS 100; 1993) that the training of special pedagogues should be open *mainly to teachers*. No reason as such was given for this more restricted requirement but it is obvious that the new economic situation has had a strong influence upon the decision. It is, in our personal opinion, a step in the wrong direction, as the above-mentioned categories involved a very favourable influence on the training of special pedagogues.

The additional programme for special pedagogues leads to a Diploma in Special Education after a three-semester training which amounts to 60 credits. It is divided into four different lines, for pupils of all ages:

* pupils with special learning problems;
* developmentally disabled pupils;
* deaf and hard-of-hearing pupils;
* blind and visually impaired pupils.

In addition the special pedagogues are offered additional courses of 20 to 40 credits. These courses involve:

* speech and language problems;
* mobility impairment;
* autism;
* socio-emotional problems;
* multi-handicaps.

It has already been decided to offer a master's degree in special education, but the requirements are not completely determined yet. In comparison with many other countries it seems as if the programme offered today does not need to be greatly extended.

In all programmes the new role for special pedagogues is strongly emphasized. It is made obvious to the students that their future work will involve:

* teaching of special needs pupils, both in small groups and/or in regular classroom situations;
* teamwork with different combinations of school staff;
* an important role as a consultant to colleagues and parents.

CLOSING REMARKS

As in most countries in Europe, policy concerning special education has changed over the years. For the moment the official attitude is reasonably favourable, but owing to the strained economic situation there have been some cutbacks during the last three years. This is of course regrettable, especially as the majority of special needs pupils are placed in regular classes. It is also a challenge, however, as the special pedagogues can no longer spend their days in a small room with single children or small groups. This was too often the case in the past.

Legislation and official policy very clearly indicate that we should create a school for all, with no exceptions. We have not yet achieved this and there is still a long way to go. We might never reach that goal but it is necessary to strive in that direction. It calls for a constant readiness for change and in this the special pedagogues are key persons.

REFERENCES

Bladini, U.B. (1990) *Från Hjälpskolelärare till Förändringsagent* (From Special Schoolteacher to an Agent for Change). Gothenburg: Acta Universitatis Gothoburgensis.

Blomberg, I. (1934) *Sinnesslövårdens Historia i Korta Drag* (The History of Services for the Mentally Retarded). Stockholm: Beckmans.

Egidius, H. (1978) *Pedagogiska Utvecklingslinjer* (Pedagogical Developmental Patterns). Stockholm: Esselte.

Lpo 94, 1994 års Läroplan för det Obligatoriska Skolväsendet (1994) *National Curriculum for the Compulsory School*. Stockholm: Ministry of Education.

Malmö School of Education (1990) *Lokal plan för specialpedagogisk påbyggnadsutbildning* (Local study plan, additional line for special pedagogues; translation by J. Rosenqvist). 1990–05–29.

Rust, V.D. (1988) 'Sweden'. In G.T. Kurian (ed.) *World Education Encyclopedia, Vol. III*. New York: Fact on File Publications. pp. 1171–82.

SFS (Swedish Statute Book) 1990:745 (1990) *Förordning om Ändring i Högskoleförordningen.* (Concerning Change of the University Ordinance). Stockholm: Norstedts.

SFS (Swedish Statute Book) 1993:100 (1993) *Högskoleförordning* (University Ordinance). Stockholm: Norstedts.

SIA (Skolans Inre Arbete) (1976) *The Inner Work of the School* (Regeringens Proposition 1975/76:39). Governmental proposal.

Statistisk Årsbok 1990 (1991) (Statistical Abstracts of Sweden 1990). Stockholm: Statistiska Centralbyrån.

Statistiska Meddelanden (1991) Grundsärskolan, Särskolan och Specialskolan 1990–91 (Statistical Messages. Comprehensive Schools, Schools for Mentally Retarded and Special Schools 1990–91). Stockholm: Statistiska Centralbyrån.

Name Index

Subject Index

analytical competence, and teacher training   89
Aptitude and Instruction Interactions (AIIs)   97–8
Association for Special Education (ASE)   101
ATEE (Association for Teacher Education in
   Europe)   x, 6, 19

Basque country   14–15
Belgium   15
blind pupils see visually impaired pupils
British Ability Scales   97
British Dyslexia Association   94

concept systems, and mathematics   111
Council of Europe   4
Council for National Academic Awards
   (CNAA)   129
Czech Republic   ix–x, 6–7, 15, 119–26
   age of compulsory education   6
   and disability   119–21
      categories of   7
   'National Plan of Provisions for People with a
      Handicap'   121
   Night School for Mentally Handicapped
      Adults   124
   and parents   123
   Psychopedics Association   124
   and schools   121–2
   special schools   6
   and teacher education   122–3, 125

deaf pupils see hearing impaired pupils
Denmark   7, 15
   age of compulsory education   7
   categories of disability   7
   categorization of pupils   54
   and the folkeskole   7
Department for Education (DfE), grants for in-
   service training   130

Department of Education and Science (DES)
   award-bearing courses   131
   grants for in-service training   130
disability, use of term   4–5
disabled students, mathematics for   106–7
distance education   132
   see also open learning
dyslexia
   L type   98
   and hemispheric alluding stimulation (HAS)   98
   in Lithuania   83
   P type   98
   specific developmental dyslexia (SDD)   94–105
Dyslexia Institute   94
Dyslexia Institute Guild   101

EADTU (European Association of Distance
   Teaching Universities)   18
EASE (European Association for Special
   Education)   ix, x
Eastern Europe
   Open University collaboration in   23–4
   see also Czech Republic; Hungary; Poland
educational psychologists, in Italy   55
emotional and behavioural difficulties (EBD),
      pupils with
   in Italy   55, 59
   in Lithuania   76, 79, 81
   and mathematics   110
   training needs of teachers of   87–93
England and Wales
   initial teacher training   128–9
   managing SEN training   37–45
   professional development for special needs
      education   127–37
   see also United Kingdom
equal opportunities   4
   and 'values' education   18–19
ERASMUS programme   x, 15

Nightingales on the Nile "Um ko Tum"
(= female Egyptian singer - '60